Never Again

Moving On from Narcissistic Abuse and Other Toxic Relationships

Dr Sarah Davies

Matador
9 Priory Business Park,
Wistow Road, Kibworth Beauchamp,
Leicestershire. LE8 0RX
Tel: 0116 279 2299
Email: books@troubador.co.uk
Web: www.troubador.co.uk/matador
Twitter: @matadorbooks

ISBN 978 1838590 314

British Library Cataloguing in Publication Data.
A catalogue record for this book is available from the British Library.

Printed and bound in Great Britain by 4edge Limited
Typeset in 11pt Sabon by Troubador Publishing Ltd, Leicester, UK

Matador is an imprint of Troubador Publishing Ltd

A special thank you to all the people I have worked with who have inspired with their bravery, resilience and self-belief and who have encouraged me to write this book.

This book is dedicated to all those who find the strength, courage and humility to face narcissistic abuse and take the steps to grow, recover and move on... however painful, difficult or frightening that may be at times. You are an inspiration and may you continue to grow and shine.

Contents

1.
Coming to terms with having a narcissist in your life

No doubt, if you are reading this book it's because you already have some interest in, or awareness of narcissism. If you are reading this book because you have experienced being in a relationship with a narcissist or have experienced narcissistic abuse then I would suggest that an important fundamental first step in recovery from this kind of abuse is to understand more about the nature of narcissism. What it looks like, what it sounds like, the origins of narcissistic traits and so on... The first few chapters will cover an overview of this. This book does not focus mostly on the narcissist though. After an overview of narcissism, the focus then shifts to you and your recovery. The aim is to provide information, tips and techniques to help you manage your relationship, to break free from the narcissists spell, to learn how you can protect yourself and to avoid being negatively affected by narcissistic abuse in the future. Too much focus on the narcissist is itself a big part of the problem. Recovery starts when you begin to bring the focus back to yourself.

For many people, starting to awaken to and coming to realise that a person in their personal or professional life is a narcissist can be quite a shock. It can be the beginning of a somewhat difficult and confusing process. The aim of this book is really to help support you along this process of recovery. Some ideas and suggestions are included to help guide your recovery and healing, as well as to help ensure you are not vulnerable to experiencing narcissistic abuse again. Part of this may include developing awareness of, and perhaps starting to break any patterns of attraction to this kind of relational dynamic in the first place.

I have experienced narcissistic abuse first hand. I have walked through this recovery journey myself and now, as a Counselling Psychologist and Trauma Therapist, alongside the many clients I work with in my private practice. A large part of the clinical work I do is specialising in helping people identify, work through, manage and recover from narcissistic abuse.

Narcissism: there is a lot of it around. As humans, we naturally seek to make sense of, and ascribe meaning to our experience. Making sense of a narcissists behaviour is not always easy though, especially at the beginning. Learning what you can about narcissism, including its origins, can really help with starting to process your experience specific to narcissistic abuse. However, a word of caution… As it dawns on us that this is perhaps what we have been, or still are experiencing, there is a danger of becoming 'stuck' at this stage. Stuck at the stage of analytically trying to work it all out. Stuck at trying to understand why he/she/they have acted in the ways that they have. This is quite paralysing. This is a stage of desperately trying to analytically and cognitively work out and understand how or why this has happened. The questions we are often left with include:

> *How could this person do this? How can they be so wonderful some of the time and so cruel at other times? They were so lovely at the beginning… what happened? Did they ever really love me? Are they even capable of love? What did I do wrong? What's wrong with me? How could they 'switch' so much? How can they be so venomous? Why did they do this to me? Will this ever change? How could I not see it? Why did I not*

listen to the warning signs? Is it my fault? Am I responsible? What did I do? and so on...

It is absolutely a normal and necessary part of the process to spend time relaying your past experiences in relation to the narcissist, trying to work through the chronology of events, as well as the progression and demise of the relationship. This is simply our minds natural inclination to want to make sense of all that has happened, to process information and to ascribe meaning to our experience. It is our minds innate mechanism to understand and process our experiences. In the quest for very human and natural sense making, you will likely want to find the clues and the answers to the many questions you may have. This is completely understandable and very much a part of the early stages of recovery. It aids to some extent, coming to terms with narcissistic abuse. It can also be very helpful for us to learn from. We may look back and recognise in hindsight the signs and the clues that were there... The snidey comments, the missed dates, the inconsistencies, the 'hooks', the lies, the jealousy, the selfishness, the inconsiderations, the 'gaslighting' and more... This is all helpful and very much an important part of the recovery process. Many people in the shock and trauma of narcissistic abuse find themselves locked on for hours relaying and thinking this through. To some extent this is a normal, expected and an essential part of the process. However, at some point, it is really important to recognise the difficult fact that, in reality, *you may never have the answers to all your questions.* And the simple reason for this is because:

It is impossible to use logic to try and understand completely illogical actions

Nonsensical behaviour is simply what we have with any narcissist. So whilst it is important and helpful that we try and work through and seek to understand some of our experience in relation to the narcissist – ultimately we begin to come to a point where we start to reconcile that we may never know, or understand, or get the answers to the many questions we are left with. I often see people become stuck at the stage of trying to work it all out. Sometimes people are stuck there for a very long time. This is unfortunately not recovery in action. It's being stuck in illness, obsession, analysis paralysis, shock and trauma. You cannot understand illogical people and their illogical actions with logic. Instead, in order to move on, you must begin the difficult process of reconciliation of being left with unanswered questions along with accepting all the feelings that go with that.

In reality this process can feel like a painful dance and at times, feel like a seemingly endless and horrific tango – two steps forward, two steps back... whilst wearing shoes that are two sizes too small! Please know that this is all part of the recovery process. You will probably wrestle again and again with wanting to understand and make sense of all that has happened. This is all very natural and understandable. This process in itself is necessary to some extent. There will be good days, and other times it will most likely feel like an overwhelming struggle. But ultimately, you will start to see that it's futile to persevere with trying to make complete sense of what is essentially somebody else's nonsense. It will likely come up again and again at times throughout the healing process. Less so, in time however, as you learn to sit more comfortably with the not-knowing and to accept this more readily. This *will* get easier. With the right tools, support and therapy work, you can and will feel better.

Importantly, if you are arriving/have arrived at the realisation you are currently, or have been involved with a narcissist, chances are you have probably already been through enough. That is one of the reasons why it is so crucial from this point forward, that you learn to be very gentle, kind, forgiving and compassionate with yourself. For some of us, our self-esteem may be so low, or we may have experienced so much abuse that the concept of self-care reads a bit alien at the moment. That's OK. This will be covered in later chapters, but for now, this means recognising that:

a) you've had a tough and difficult experience, and that on a weekly or day by day or even moment by moment basis from now, you can;

b) begin to tune into whatever is a good thing to do for yourself and to focus more on what *you* need – all that is simply kind, loving, supportive and healing for yourself.

Just take a moment now to pause here and just notice what it is like *right now* having just read that point about the importance of self care and self compassion. *What do you notice within yourself? What are your thoughts or feelings about that? Are you keen to skip past this bit? Did you automatically dismiss this point as too basic – do you feel like you already know all this? Or is it that you don't really get what the concept of self-care really means right now? Are you usually too busy putting other peoples needs before your own? Does the idea of being kind or compassionate to yourself bring anything else up? If so, what? Does it feel selfish? Does it help to acknowledge that perhaps you may be too hard on yourself sometimes? Or is this difficult to consider right now? Is there any room for improvement?* There usually is.

We will cover more about self-care, our inner self-talk, kindness and compassion in later chapters as these are important fundamentals in fostering a healthy relationship with ourselves. It is also a crucial component in recovery from narcissistic abuse and an effective shield that protects us from getting into and staying in abusive relationships again in the future. For now though, self care may mean reaching out to friends, talking to a therapist, taking a relaxing lavender bath, treating yourself to something nice, taking a spa day with friends, spending time with people who care about you, walking in nature, enjoying a round of golf, reading a self-help book or positive literature, eating well, seeing a show with friends or family, shopping, volunteering, yoga, resting, meditating, or otherwise trying anyway in which to be gentle and kind to yourself.

Many people who find themselves in relationship with narcissists are actually some of the kindest, most understanding, forgiving, caring and loving people you could possibly wish to meet. Usually though, with a focus on caring, loving and attending to everybody else's wants and needs before their own. So chances are you already actually know how to love, be kind and care – because you do this for others. Recovery starts with fine-tuning this forgiveness, kindness, care and compassion to **yourself.**

Healthy relationships begin first and foremost with truly developing a healthy and loving relationship with yourself

Once we have this in place, all other relationships become much easier. This is healthy relationships in the right order.

Being involved with a narcissist feels a lot like being on a roller coaster... there are highs and lows... it's exciting and fun at times... absolutely horrific and frightening at others... Just like a rollercoaster ride, if you stay on for long enough, it will leave you sick... If you're reading this book there is every chance that you've had enough of being on this ride. The aim of this book is to help you develop the insight and self-help tools to get off, stay off, recover and move on with your life.

This book is written with the simple intention of sharing my knowledge and experience to help you and others. There may be some things you like and agree with and I hope find helpful, there may be things that you don't. You may find some parts difficult reading. I would like to just offer encouragement to take whatever it is you find helpful and I truly wish you all the very best with your recovery journey.

Best wishes,
Dr. Sarah Davies

2. Narcissus and Echo – the tragedy

The word 'narcissism' comes from Greek, specifically from Greek Mythological character, Narcissus. The story of Narcissus and Echo captures a tragic relationship that highlights the dynamic seen between narcissists and those, the 'Echos', who are typically drawn to them.

Narcissus was a charismatic and handsome hunter, with a reputation for breaking the hearts of many by rejecting their love. Never satisfied, he was arrogant and aloof. The story goes, that as punishment for his ongoing disdain and arrogance, the Goddess of Revenge – Nemesis, casts a spell on him, where he would fall in love with the very next person he sees. Soon after, one day in fierce heat, Narcissus, tired and drained from his enthusiastic hunting, decides to take some rest by a still lake. As he takes a drink from the lake he sees an image in the water and immediately falls deeply in love – with his own reflection. From that moment forward, Narcissus remains completely enthralled and captivated with his own image and all that for which he is himself admired. He does not realise at all that he is in fact in love with his own idealistic image. And so he begins, a futile pursuit for this unobtainable love.

Echo, beautiful and sweet, it is said, was disciplined by Goddess Juno for being too talkative. As punishment, Goddess Juno deprived Echo of her ability to express herself directly, tragically being left unable to say anything on her own. She effectively loses her own voice and instead is only able to utter the last words of others, finishing sentences, yet unable to start them.

When she meets Narcissus she becomes completely infatuated with him. She desperately tries to reach out to him, to connect, to communicate with him and have him hear her, see her, acknowledge and love her... but she can't. And he can't. Echo desperately and painfully longs for the attention and affections of Narcissus, however he remains completely fixated on himself. Narcissus continues to reject Echo and her love, yet undeterred she goes on to spend her life obsessed and consumed by her pursuit of the impossible with Narcissus. Echo eventually disappears so all that is left of her is a limited voice of others. Narcissus also eventually wastes away in time with the obsessive love he has for himself – essentially dying from the agony of never being able to ever have his object of desire. Both are tragically left discontent, in pain, heartbroken and alone.

The story of Narcissus and Echo really captures the futile pursuit and obsession around the fantasy of 'love' from both sides.

"It probably started sooner than I cared to acknowledge. In the early months of us being together; the inconsistencies and verbal abuse. There were several times when I would be hit with an absolute torrent of verbal abuse. Being called selfish (hardly!?!), mad, even being called the abuser... a narcissist... it sounds crazy now, but I just took it. I was actually in a state of shock and disbelief as to how he could go from being so lovely, to so utterly vile. I guess I just couldn't see what was going on. I was blinded.

In hindsight, this abuse would often come at times when I was wanting to go out with friends, trying to enjoy a girls night from time to time. To start with he would wish me a nice evening, often buying me gifts before I left. My friends would be envious – their partners didn't do that, they'd say. I see the gifts and the timing of them now as quite sinister, because my friends would say how sweet it was of him to get me nice things and then they couldn't understand if I would say, later on in the evening, that he was being horrible to me. They sort of dismissed it as this is a lovely man who buys nice gifts?!?! He was a wonderful boyfriend to the outside. I very quickly just kept the bullying to myself. I realise now, that was what he wanted. Anyway, the evenings would start well, then during the night I'd get calls and messages where he would get increasingly abusive and irrational. I'd be accused of not caring about him, leaving him, being selfish, flirting, being promiscuous. None of it was true at all, but I strangely felt very guilty! I would feel terrible like I had done something wrong. I was scared. I'd even question myself if I had!!? Then I would be the one desperately trying to make it up to him, when I hadn't even done anything. The next day I would be desperately trying to make it up to him and it would be like walking on egg shells the whole time. He would give me the silent treatment. He would sometimes act as if nothing had happened, as if he had no idea what I was talking about, or flippantly blame it on booze. I was so blind to it all at the time. I only see it more clearly now I am out of it. I spent a lot of time in confusion. I did so much for him, but it was never enough. I lost myself, I lost my voice. I could not understand why he just couldn't appreciate me or love me back. I realise now that it's because he is not capable of that. It was futile. And I need to focus on my self worth and reminding myself that I deserve better."

Understanding the true nature and the depth of issues in narcissism, as well as those of echoism, codependency and other traits that leave us vulnerable to or being attracted to/attractive to narcissistic personality types is fundamental in recognising and ultimately accepting the futility and madness in this kind of relationship dynamic. It is important to start to separate yourself from the narcissist and vice versa. Coming to understand the other persons behaviours, mentality, struggles, issues, and so on, as their own. It is not for you, me, or anybody else to assume or take on, or take responsibility for the other persons actions, choices, pain, trauma, addictions, lies or anything else. It is important, in fact essential for their own recovery and growth, that they learn to do that for themselves. If, for whatever reason, they can't or won't, it is also crucial to know that is also not your responsibility or issue. Equally, what is your responsibility is to return the focus to your own actions, choices, behaviours, traumas, needs and wants. It's about bringing it back to you and working on yourself. Healthy detachment and working towards reclaiming a healthier balance is vital in recovery and healing from abusive relationships.

3.   What is narcissism?

Arming yourself with information about 'What is Narcissism?' is a crucial first step in learning how to recognise it. How to deal with it and recovery themes are covered later.

Narcissistic Personality Disorder (NPD) is a Cluster B psychiatric condition as defined in the DSM (Diagnostic and Statistical Manual of Mental Disorders; 2013). NPD is characterised by long-term patterns of behaviour and attitudes that centre around self-importance, disregard for others, a pathological need for admiration together with a distinct lack of empathy. People who are narcissistic have a preoccupation with achievement and success, money, power, perceived power, grandiosity and self-importance. They are manipulative and do not think twice about using or taking advantage of other people or organisations for their own selfish gains. In fact, many narcissists view others simply as commodities. They are unable to ever really experience deep, authentic relationships or connections with people.

The key features of Narcissistic Personality Disorder include:

* A strong sense of grandiosity with expectations of special treatment from others or institutions.
* Core issues of personal identity: Narcissists need constant positive regard and feedback, admiration and worship from others in order to regulate their self-esteem and sense of self.

* Displays of selfish and self-seeking actions and behaviours.
* A grandiose and exaggerated sense of self-importance – exaggerates or lies about achievements, importance, status and abilities.
* Arrogance.
* Anxiety.
* Pathological need for admiration and attention.
* Poor self-esteem and deep-seated insecurity – overcompensated for with arrogance, haughty or belittling, judgemental behaviours or comments.
* Preoccupation with ideas and fantasies about success, power, wealth, love, brilliance or looks/image.
* Sense or belief that he/she is 'special', 'different' or 'unique'.
* Strong sense of entitlement.
* Interpersonally highly manipulative and/or exploitative. Will take advantage of others for their own gains.
* Distinct lack of genuine empathy. Narcissists can actually seem very attuned to the feelings of others, but often only in anticipation of how somebody else's feelings may affect them. It is used to manipulate. Displays of empathy are ultimately geared toward their own selfish means.
* Lack of taking or accepting personal responsibility for any mistakes or wrongdoings.
* Blaming others.
* Addictions – often Narcissists have issues with excess and addiction including obsessive-compulsive tendencies, drug use, alcoholism, sex and love addiction, porn, gambling, work, etc.
* Inability to form or maintain long-term or meaningful relationships.
* Fear of and/or inability for real emotional intimacy and/or commitment.
* Aggression / aggressive behaviours. Difficulty controlling anger and rage.

(DSM, 2013).

It is worth noting that generally speaking there are two main types of narcissist.

Overt narcissism:

An **overt narcissist** is arguably much easier to spot than other more subtle forms of narcissism. They are the more stereotypically recognised example of narcissism. Overt reflects the grandiose characteristics as often depicted in Hollywood or as seen in the business world, politics and amongst the celebrity scene. Traditionally, the overt narcissist is seen as the suave, sophisticated, charismatic and confident male (although of course are also female), usually in some kind of position of power. They are often entrepreneurs, business owners, CEOs, politicians, in the arts, or in roles of strong standing and status. Wearing smart, expensive, designer, sharp or eccentric clothing, powerful fragrances and showing off a twinkle in their eye, they are the type of narcissist that will turn heads at a party. They attract and seek to surround themselves by unsuspecting admirers. They exude buckets full of charm, charisma, confidence and sex appeal. The overt narcissists often appear powerful, self-confident and self-assured, arrogant, in control, thick-skinned and indestructible on the surface. They are typically often very vain, yet fit and good-looking lotharios – although with insecurities, obsession or paranoia about their looks and image. They can also be fantastic fun, wild, have a great sense of humour, are romantic, spontaneous and seemingly loving and lovable. They may even show an enticing snippet of vulnerability in order to cast a spell over others. It is easy to see why so many people fall for the charms of the overt narcissist. They have the power to make those around them feel instantly wonderful. They also though, have the power to destroy and abuse.

It is often easier to spot an overt narcissist as they behave and treat people in a much more obvious, clear and direct way. They are almost always unashamedly self-seeking, attention seeking, high-risk behaving, selfish, manipulative addicts. They tend to be fixated on wealth, status, success, recognition, admiration and power yet at the same time are extremely sensitive to actual or perceived rejection, criticism or blame. They are overtly changeable, manipulative and often aggressive in their attempts to control others and to get what they want. Anybody who dares cross them will likely be met with the wrath of narcissistic rage. They are people who will seek to bully, harm or conversely suddenly drop associates, completely cutting off from them as if they had never existed. They are also likely to set up smear or hate campaigns in response to any rejection or fall out. They will want to cut off or punish anybody who does not worship or admire them in the way they so desperately need. Ultimately their self-serving manipulation is achieved through a variety of outlandish and incredibly subtle ways.

"I remember very clearly the first time I met John*. I was at a conference party with work. We both worked in law and so I had some friends and colleagues that already knew of him. He immediately caught my eye when he walked into the room. There must have been hundreds of people there, but I saw him, right on the other side of the room, walk through the door. He was incredibly handsome, tall, and one of the first things I noticed was his bright captivating smile. He was so attentive talking to everybody as he made his way across the room. When we were introduced I honestly felt weak at the knees. He was so handsome, charismatic, dressed good, smelt good… I couldn't believe he was there, wanting to talk to me! I was having a very bodily reaction to his mere presence. I know that might sound a bit crazy, but that was the power he had over me before we had even spoken! I'm usually quite a calm, collected and confident person but I was nervous talking to him. There was huge chemistry and energy between us both – I'd never felt anything like it. I also felt like I could see deep into his eyes, like I could see the real him. It felt like a deep connection. Looking

back, I realise now it was all so intense and at the time it was all consuming and fast became addictive, he was like my crack-cocaine hit! That night we exchanged numbers. I remember as he left, he walked out of the door and then turned back around to smile, just at me. At that moment I felt so special. Like, out of hundreds of beautiful, intelligent and interesting people at this function, he could only see me. It was mesmerising. There was a power there from day 1, no question. He text that me that evening and we quickly got into a fast-paced exchange and arranged our first date for later that week... It was intense from the very start..."

Covert Narcissism:

The **covert narcissist** is a slightly different type of presentation and one that is arguably a little more difficult to spot. In essence they share the same core pathology as the overt narcissist; having a fragile ego and self-esteem, stemming from the same kind of early damage (that will be explained shortly). However, the covert kind of narcissist comes across as more innocent and more vulnerable. They can be softly spoken, seductive, gentle, unassuming, perhaps shy, quiet, sensitive, alluring, sweet and helpful. Their core deep-seated fear and vulnerability is masked by an array of more subtle techniques of control and manipulation than are typically observed in the overt narcissist. This includes seeking to get their own needs met by coming across as caring and helpful, altruistic even. They are the rescuer. They may be very generous, buying gifts, offering funds as they use financial status to gain power and control. They manage to shame others in a variety of subtle and indirect ways. Feigning or using illness or health concerns (real or imagined) to elicit sympathy, care and concern, or guilt-tripping others as way of gaining control and getting their own needs met. Finding subtle and indirect ways to receive attention, sympathy or admiration. This can also include using love or sex as ways to control or manipulate. The covert narcissist can be quite the silent seducer. All techniques are ultimately used in order to satisfy their own narcissistic supply needs.

The covert narcissist is often the martyr who sacrifices his or her own needs for others *(and if only everybody could see and appreciate this!)*. The covert narcissist will find it easier to willingly portray their 'weaknesses' or 'vulnerabilities' than the overt narcissist. They will therefore happily relay stories of how they have been victimised, treated poorly by others, misunderstood, explain how hard done by they are and how it's everybody else fault. Again, this is all with the end goal of manipulating and controlling in order to receive the attention, affection and sympathies they so desperately need for their fragile ego state.

From my clinical practice and experience I have identified a number of main covert-type narcissistic profiles outlined in further detail here. Again, these are a little harder to detect than the out and out overt, arrogant, grandiose type narcissist more often depicted in the mainstream. They are however, equally or in some ways more troubling as often these personality types demonstrate attractive and appealing qualities yet at the same time are controlling and manipulative which only adds to a partners confusion. Please note narcissists can be more than one kind of covert profile.

The Achievement-Focused:

The achievement-focused narcissist is the kind of partner who seeks out those with status, connections and those with a desirable or important job. For the achievement-focused all that tends to matter is what you do in life as well as what you have or own. Nothing is ever enough for a materialistic narcissist. They will communicate, in a variety of ways, that whatever you achieve is never quite enough. Partners tend to be frazzled, burnt-out workaholics playing their own part in seeking contentment from the elusive arrival of 'enough'. Here, there is often a distinct disregard for emotional wellbeing. They may ignore or not recognise a partners fatigue/stress/tiredness or emotional needs, instead supporting the message via criticism and/or praise for accomplishments or display or withdrawal of love and support depending on achievements or gains.

"My partner rarely helped with things at home. I worked a big job, long hours, demanding work and I would get home exhausted and stressed. He stayed at home, just managing property that we owned. I'd get home and the house would be a mess (despite having cleaners), no food in the fridge, nothing prepared for dinner. He would expect me to work and sort out the house and cooking too. I was exhausted. Looking back I was running on empty. I don't know how I did it. But I felt compelled to please. To not let him down. I didn't want to disappoint him. If I showed him I was tired or struggling, it was like it was a weakness. When we saw friends, he would talk endlessly about how proud he was of me and all that I achieve and all the things I juggle. It felt like it became impossible to do any less."

The Victim:

The victim-type covert is quite content with showing and sharing their 'vulnerabilities' with others. They are the partner who will more or less constantly be complaining about how poorly they are or have been treated. They tend to have a history of 'bad' exes, relationships or jobs. All previous unhealthy or toxic relationships have been the other persons fault – or so they claim. They never consider their own part in any of it. More abusively, the victim-type will complain about how they are the victim in the current relationship. They will point the finger at the partner and complain about how you are not understanding or considerate enough to their needs, perhaps they may suggest they are the 'victim' of others anger, insecurities and so on. Notice how they are the victim and never keen or able to take responsibility for their part in any issue. The aim of this is to position themselves as the victim and therefore pull others into a rescuer position or guilt-trip people into actions that ultimately serve their own selfish needs and wants.

> "When I met my partner he had a good well-paid job that he found stressful but otherwise enjoyed. It gave him the status that I realise now he absolutely needed for his fragile self-esteem. About a year into the relationship he resigned and at that time we decided to relocate. Bizarrely, he then would constantly be referring to the 'fact' that he 'gave up his big job for me' and so somehow I should be eternally grateful and in debt to him for it. I never asked him to do that. It was not even my decision. I was confused about his behaviours but at the same time I started to read and learn about narcissism and controlling, abusive behaviour and realised that was a part of it. He was trying to make me feel guilty and bad. Our relationship started to deteriorate and I, having reached my limits, decided I could not take any more of his controlling ways and I somehow managed to find the strength to leave. I hear he still blames me for his career move and not only that, now paints me out to be the bad guy by suggesting we moved for him and then I left and abandoned him!. As far as I can see, he gets a number of gains from portraying himself as the 'victim'. Friends and family of his rally round and offer sympathy and all bad mouth me as the evil, mad one. He is the victim – poor him. It's rubbish – it's narcissism".

The Rescuer/Saviour:

The rescuer/saviour kind of narcissist is actually one I see and hear a lot about in my private practice. Interestingly, partners have seem to have met or gotten into a relationship with a rescuer/

saviour covert narcissist at times of their own vulnerability. Perhaps at a time of a recent break-up or divorce, bereavement or particularly stressful time at work. The rescuer almost certainly tends to appear at a time when we are at our most vulnerable. They appear like a knight in shining armour ready to care, protect and look after a new partner. This is a variation of love-bombing – effectively care-bombing – and frankly if timed when we are in need it is welcome and easy to succumb to at the time. However, just as with love-bombing in the early stages, this ultimately leads to controlling their partners in time.

"I had not long been divorced when I met Michael*. It had been an emotionally abusive relationship and a bitter long drawn out divorce. I was exhausted. Then along came Michael and I couldn't believe my luck! He was romantic, caring and doting. He would buy me gifts, come and cook for me after work, in fact he would pick me up to and from work, he helped me get back on my feet financially. Soon he was paying household bills at his insistence and then he moved in within 6 months of us meeting. Looking back I was so beaten from my previous relationship I pretty much didn't even have the energy say 'no' to any of his suggestions. I just let him do whatever he wanted to. To be honest, it was quite welcome to have somebody so loving and caring at the time as that was quite opposite to how things had ended up with my previous partner. But in time, as I started to feel better and stronger, I started to realise how utterly controlling he was. He would want, in fact I'd say need, to do almost everything for me. I could hardly breathe. If I ever insisted I wanted to buy my own food or travel to work alone he'd become suspicious, argumentative, upset or resentful. He was incredibly needy. He would guilt-trip a lot. I started to experience bad anxiety and panic attacks as I realised I had ended up in another abusive relationship – he had jumped on me when I was vulnerable. It was then that I sought professional

help to end these patterns once and for all. I thought I am not going through all this again!"

The Addict:

Addiction is a common trait in narcissists and one that is usually fairly easy to spot in potential partners. However, I have included this in the overt profiles as it can be an infliction that is used to manipulate and hook partners in with a slightly more subtle way. By this I mean the addict who will look to partners to help them, rescue them, fix them or in any other way take responsibility for their actions. Addiction in any form is essentially narcissistic behaviour. Addicts in their active addiction are selfish and self-seeking with the focus being on obtaining and indulging in their next hit – regardless of drug of choice. This involves a whole host of manipulation in order to maintain their addiction. The addicted narcissist will seek to pull partners into a position of rescuer, carer or fixer and usually guilt-trip them into doing so. They will often use a victim position to facilitate their active addiction too.

"When I found out Lucy had cheated I was devastated. Prior to that we had, as far as I was concerned, a great relationship! She was beautiful, smart, funny, we did lots of things together, travelled, etc. I found text messages on her phone and confronted her about it. At first she flew into a rage saying that I was the one who was out of order for not trusting her and looking at her phone. I felt terrible. At the time I felt really bad and guilty for looking at her phone. She made me feel like I was the mad one. She told me it had been a one off because I had been away on a work trip and she had been left feeling lonely. She basically was blaming me and saying that if I hadn't left her for a week then she wouldn't have had to cheat. I told her I was leaving. Then she cried hysterically and begged me to stay, that she was sorry and had made a mistake. She insisted she

needed help and was going to seek therapy and would never do it again. I felt for her. I could see she was in pain. I guess I wanted to believe her. I felt sorry for her and also felt a part guilty. We tried again. She went to a therapist for one session but came back saying they were rubbish and that was it. The months went by. The trust had gone and three months later I found a receipt for a daytime hotel so I knew she was still cheating and still lying to me. It had to end then."

The Psychosomatic:

The psychosomatic narcissist uses aches and pains, illness and health anxieties – either real or imagined – to ensure the focus and attention is on them. Illness and complaints of symptoms are used in order to control and manipulate or even to keep partners from leaving them.

"When I came to terms that I was in a relationship with a highly needy and manipulative partner I set about making plans to leave them. Whenever I did though, they would feign illness or actually even get very sick. It was only when this happened after the 5th or 6th time I tried to leave them that a friend pointed out this was a clear pattern. They had even arranged surgery on one occasion! They were seeking to guilt-trip me into not leaving however when I saw this very manipulative pattern I left immediately and never looked back!"

Some narcissists will oscillate between overt and covert varieties. By the way, either kind of narcissist will likely tend to have a history of 'psycho-exes/friends/colleagues' and therefore make out they have consistently been the victim. However if this relationship disaster/victimhood pattern exists, I would argue that there is one common denominator in the mix – and that is the person to steer clear of!

"When I first met Andrew, my first impressions were that he was a very sweet, kind and patient man. He seemed well liked amongst colleagues and had a good sense of humour. He was quite a quiet, softly spoken man – he seemed nice. He talked openly about difficulties he had in his life, he was divorced, had been an alcoholic but through the 12 step programme had been sober and abstinent for over 10 years at that point. At first I found him caring. He came across as open and honest, vulnerable even. We connected instantly.

I was recently single and I guess I was feeling quite lonely at the time. Andrew came along and very quickly was bombarding me with compliments, gifts, dinners and evenings out, even romantic breaks away. Although he wasn't really my type, I accepted. I guess I enjoyed the attention and the romance of it. He was quite besotted with me and I was flattered. Looking back I can see that he quickly grew attached to me, perhaps even becoming quite obsessed about me. He soon told me he loved me. He said he'd had never felt anything like this before. I can see now, with help from my therapist, that this relationship was based on fantasy right from the start – for him for sure, but for both of us to some extent.

At the time I was a bit out of sorts and didn't have the strength to stop things… I felt like he kind of pushed me into a relationship I wasn't really ready for, or even wanted. Even though I told him I wanted to take my time, he never listened to me – he never heard me. He always knew best. It was kind of like he believed he knew what was better for me, more than I did. I found that quite annoying and disrespectful really – as if I was not capable of making decisions for myself. But at the time, I was quite passive and just went along with it. He could be quite overbearing. At the time, though, it was refreshing to have somebody take charge so I just went with it. A few months in and I was already starting to feel quite suffocated. He wanted to do everything together. Another few months *down the line we were practically living together, but I knew I wanted out. I felt like I couldn't breathe.*

He had quickly become controlling, wanting to know where I was, who with, getting grumpy and giving me the silent treatment whenever I went out without him or if I had done anything 'wrong' . Sometimes I didn't know what I was supposed to have done. He wouldn't talk or explain why he was annoyed with me either. That was very anxiety-provoking for me. I realise now that his behaviour was abusive. He wouldn't give me any personal space. Even if we were arguing, he wouldn't let me leave the room or the house to calm down. I think he actually couldn't tolerate me being away from him. I realise now he was incredibly controlling. By his own admission, he wasn't good at being on his own. When I tried to end things, he would either completely ignore me, denying that anything was wrong, or somehow turn things around as if I was incapable of being able to make a decision. I would then actually doubt myself. I doubted whether I really did want to leave him. I didn't know what I thought or felt anymore. He would also make vague threats, saying things like "OK, you leave... and then you see what happens". That used to really panic me and paralysed by fear, I would end up not going anywhere. It was awful. I felt trapped. I was just left worrying and imagining all the 'what ifs'. I know it sounds crazy, but I tried to leave many times before I was eventually able to. Every time, there would be some excuse or drama.

Many times I tried to leave, he would suddenly become very ill, bed-ridden and guilt-trip me through his ailments into not leaving him. I'd be stuck again, feeling duty bound to look after him. I was such a nervous wreck at that time. He used illness and feigned health concerns to stop me from leaving. In the end I started to realise the pattern that every time I was close to leaving, instead I would be at the doctors or a hospital appointment with him or nursing him at home. It was mad.

Whenever I mentioned or tried to talk to mutual acquaintances about this, I was left feeling very misunderstood. It was a very lonely time. Nobody believed me, because he came across as such a different person to them compared to what I saw behind closed doors. I don't think people actually believed me or wanted to get involved. On many occasions I witnessed him suddenly switch if somebody else was around. Everybody seemed to think he was lovely and kind and that I was lucky to be with him. It seriously made me doubt my own judgement. I thought I must have it all wrong. People thought it was me and that I was being the horrible one. He would even sometimes 'joke' to his friends that I was mentally unwell, that I had a personality disorder, that I was the mad one. It makes me sick to think of that now, it was so horrifically controlling and abusive. He was projecting. He is a narcissist. I see that very clearly now. During that time though I could feel myself changing, I didn't feel like me. My self-esteem and confidence was really affected. I had quickly lost touch with many of my friends. I was exhausted.

Things just got to the point where I had simply had enough. I have no idea where I found the strength from, but one day I just knew I could not take anymore. I packed up and left. I felt better in myself and more like me again, almost immediately! My recovery has continued since then and I am so glad I got away. I feel like me again. I am free."

THE NARCISSIST SCALE:

Narcissistic traits sit on a spectrum. There is a scale of narcissism. Just because somebody exhibits some selfish behaviours sometimes, it does not necessarily mean they have a raging narcissistic personality disorder. At the extreme end of narcissism is narcissistic personality disorder (NPD). These are individuals with a frightening lack of empathy, or ability to relate, connect to others or to feel emotions in the way other people do. They really are able to switch off from their feelings so as not to experience any real empathy, regret, remorse, personal responsibility or consideration for others. At the other end of the spectrum lies most of the rest of us. Most people are capable of *some* narcissistic traits *sometimes*. Arguably we all have a little narcissism in us and are capable at the very least of the potential to be selfish, self-seeking or self-absorbed at times. I think it is a little narcissist in nature to believe you have the power to change, please or fix other people/partners. We do not have that power and control over anybody else. Codependents, echoists, even therapists and healthcare workers can sometimes identify a narcissistic tendency in their desires to help, rescue or repair the wounds in others. Recognising this in ourselves is important. Narcissists usually struggle to self-reflect honestly. Self-reflection is essential for humility, honesty and personal growth.

Whilst the desire and belief that we have the power to help or control others does have hints of narcissism in its essence, it is not the same as full-blown narcissism. There is hope and potential for positive growth and recovery from narcissistic traits when there is capacity for honest, self-awareness, the *genuine* ability to reflect on ones own behaviours and desires and to consider the potential impact that has on others. There is a chance of change in narcissistic tendencies if we are able to experience empathy, regret and genuine compassion for others. True narcissists are less likely to be able to experience any of these qualities (although the best narcissists will be more than capable of faking this!). Positive change, growth and healing from narcissistic traits also requires a strong and consistent motivation to do so. Another thing that is needed for change is the ability to take personal responsibility. Most true NPDs are unable to take responsibility for themselves or their actions, preferring instead to blame everybody else and to pull others into the role of taking responsibility on their behalf.

The reality is, that in Western societies at least, narcissism is rife. There are lots of it out there. The odds are you will have already come across narcissists in school, at work, in your family, at university, in your love life, on the dating scene, whatever your age, gender or sexual orientation. The important thing now for your own recovery and sanity, is to firstly learn about narcissism. Learn how to spot the signs and perhaps more importantly then learn how to *take notice* of the warning signs. In cases where having involvement with the narcissist is unavoidable, learn how to best manage this, working on your own boundaries in order to protect and look after yourself. This book aims to cover practical tools and tips in order to help with this.

Reflection point:

* What are the key characteristics of a narcissist?
* What traits or characteristics do you recognise in the narcissist/s in your life?
* What is the difference between an overt and covert narcissist?
* How might you identify an overt and a covert narcissist?
* What is the difference between Narcissistic Personality Disorder (NPD) and Narcissistic traits?

THE ORIGINS OF NARCISSISM

One of the first steps in recovering from narcissistic abuse and breaking any pattern of being drawn to this kind of dynamic is to firstly develop a solid understanding of narcissism. This includes the reasons why narcissists are the way they are, knowing that it is not personal, that it is not something that is likely to ever change, that it is not your fault or responsibility, spotting the signs a mile off, as well as learning how to manage your interactions with them whilst keeping yourself safe. Understanding more about the nature and the origins of narcissism is a good, helpful start for your own processing following a difficult or abusive experience. When we have been subjected to narcissistic abuse, we are often left with much confusion and a whole host of difficult and unanswered questions. Our minds will naturally be trying to make sense of why and how certain things have happened or why or how somebody could do the things that this person has done. As mentioned earlier, some understanding can assist the processing of your own experience. However it is likely that you will be left with some questions that you may never find any answers to. It can be helpful though, particularly in the early stages of recovery, to develop an understanding of why a narcissist behaves in the way he or she does. It can help you to make sense of how and why some people are damaged in this way. Please note though, this is not about sympathising, making excuses or justifying the abusive behaviours or actions of the narcissist. It is about helping *you* to begin *your* journey of healing and recovery by gaining more insight into this personality type. The narcissist is damaged and psychologically unwell.

There are a number of factors in the origins and development of narcissistic personality. Some evidence suggests that there is actually some genetic heritability of narcissistic personality disorder (Paris, 2014; Torgersep Lygren, Oien, Skre, Onstad, Edvardsen, Tambs & Kringlen, 2000). The research works of Dr. William Walsh (2014) also reveals key biochemical markers that associate with anti-social and behavioural problems thus suggesting an element of individual biochemistry may also be in the mix – this can also be hereditary. Ultimately though, I believe our environment and early childhood experiences are the most significant influence on the breeding and development of narcissistic personality disorder.

It is understood that two extreme and contrasting types of parenting and childhood experience relate to the development of narcissistic traits or personality types. One is experiencing significant neglect or abuse as a young child. The other is quite the opposite and involves a childhood of over-parenting, or having family or caregivers who have consistently over-complimented, over-estimated and over-exaggerated the abilities of the child. Either extreme is unhealthy and has been shown to relate to the development of narcissistic personality and traits.

EARLY CHILDHOOD NEGLECT AND ABUSE

When a baby is born they are obviously completely vulnerable and totally reliant on their primary caregiver whom is most often, but not always, their parent. Any baby will be relying on their primary caregiver to recognise and respond to all of their primary care needs in the early stages of their life, and thus, support their physical, emotional and psychological development. With limited capacity yet to speak, communicate or articulate their own wants or needs, a baby will simply and instinctively cry in order to try and get their wants and needs attended to. The baby screams, and in an ideal scenario, a mother, father, or other primary caregiver will recognise and respond appropriately to that need or demand. Whether it be out of pain and discomfort, for food, for comfort, to seek a sense of safety and security or anything else they need. Generally, through direct experience, as those core needs are responded to effectively and appropriately, a baby will experience the beginnings of a secure or 'good enough' attachment and bond with their parent or caregiver. We absolutely do not need 'perfect parenting'. Good enough parenting is a caregiver who is able to attune to the child enough. This in turn, fundamentally impacts and shapes the psychological and emotional development of the child. Narcissists have usually experienced some kind of significant disruption in care during these early stages. Please note: narcissists are <u>not</u> bred from a parent or caregiver who for whatever reason does not immediately respond to every single one of the child's needs! Being a parent is an incredibly challenging and difficult task. Parenting and a parental bond only ever needs to be 'good enough' – it does not need to be in any way 'perfect'. (I do not believe there is such a thing as a perfect childhood anyway, but for normal development, it just needs to be enough).

The significant disruptions in this early stage that can lead to the development of narcissism include significant and/or long-term neglect or having unstable attachment figures. This can be due to a parent being narcissistic themselves, being unavailable, preoccupied, or perhaps struggling with their own mental health or issues with addiction. It can also be a result of a very harsh, punitive or unsupportive parenting style. Sometimes, this is certainly not intentional a lot of the time either. Perhaps a parent became ill in the early years and was unable to care as well as she/he might liked to have. It can also be the case that the youngest in the family can struggle more with getting their needs met appropriately as the family are simply tied up with managing several other, older children. I have also seen cases where one parent is suspected as perhaps being on the autistic spectrum and so some of the interaction styles have been modelled, that resemble narcissism in some ways. Usually, consistent and supportive family life can be enough to repair any earlier issues.

Young children are ego-centric, meaning they have not yet developed a 'theory of mind' (Piaget, 1997; 1954). They have not yet developed the perspective to recognise that other people have different internal experiences, thoughts, feelings or needs to their own. Babies and children at this stage experience others as simply an extension of themselves. They believe that whatever they are experiencing – thoughts or feelings – others are having the same experience. They assume that others around them know and understand their internal experience or needs. Children of a young age have not yet developed the capacity to recognise a separation or distinction as to where they and others begin and end. This includes recognising that their experience may be different to somebody else's.

The very beginnings of narcissism often lies at this early pivotal developmental stage. If we, as very young children, have our basic primary needs met, responded to, attuned to and attended to in a supportive and appropriate way, we then successfully progress through this emotional and psychological developmental milestone. We usually go on to be well-adjusted, considerate, responsible, caring adults. Ideally, children experience enough consistent unconditional love, trust, positive regard and feedback that it in turn supports the emergence of healthy self-esteem and key reciprocal relational skills. With a secure base, we are able to develop enough inner psychological security to be able to care for ourselves in a variety of ways. With consistent care and emotional support, we learn to recognise and consider the needs of ourselves and others and in time develop into responsible, caring and considerate, emotionally mature adolescents and adults. Narcissists have often not had the most ideal early childhood environment for this development to occur. They therefore get stuck at the ego-centric (effectively selfish/self-seeking) stage and are unable to consider other peoples feelings or experience. In the absence of unconditional love or regard, they instead learn shame, anger and a deep sense of worthlessness. Because early primitive needs were not attended to appropriately, narcissists are in essence, emotionally stunted at this developmental stage. They have a deep sense of shame, distrust and fear. They have not learnt to appropriately consider other peoples positions, needs or wants. Instead they are fixated on getting their own needs and wants met. By the time they reach adulthood, narcissist personality types are rather hell-bent on getting these needs met in whichever ever way they can. By then, they have usually well learnt to manipulate to get their way. The sense of shame, distrust, anger and fear that forms the basis of a narcissistic personality, sets the scene for the range of active defences that are all relied upon in order to keep the narcissist away from truly getting in touch with any of their pain and shame. These deeply difficult feelings are instead overcompensated with by arrogance and grandiose fantasies.

So essentially, this emotional damage comes from not having had early primary care needs met. In reality, this can simply relate to regularly not being fed when hungry as a baby or toddler, or being left when upset or crying and having needs consistently and significantly neglected. The parents of narcissists for whatever reason, have often been unable to mirror healthy connection, attention, warmth and appropriate responsiveness. Perhaps they have their own mental health issues, unresolved trauma, unmet needs, wounds, addictions or preoccupations that has prevented them from being able to support a healthy or consistent emotional and psychological connection with their child. Parenting trends have really changed over the years. A few decades ago it was more common advice to leave young children to cry until they were able to soothe themselves and quieten down. Our understanding now is that when babies stop crying, it can be that they have simply given up the hope of being responded to. An ongoing and significant amount of these sorts of experiences in the early years can be enough to begin to shape a narcissistic personality. It may or may not have been through intentional neglect or abuse.

The sorts of backgrounds that I have seen quite commonly with narcissists include; parents/family/caregivers who, during the early stages were either absent, alcoholic/addicted or otherwise inconsistent in their connection or parenting abilities. Sometimes the parent or parents have their own unresolved trauma or emotional issues. It can be that one parent is suspected as being on the autistic spectrum and struggled to connect emotionally to the child. Often there are strong ideas, perhaps culturally or otherwise about parenting styles – there seems a link to narcissism and erratic, harsh, 'tough' parenting. Sometimes the family of origin with the narcissists I have worked with has also included being a child to struggling parents, such as to very young, immature parents, with mental health problems, or being the youngest in a large family. It has also included growing up in very chaotic or abusive households, for example, parents / couples arguing and fighting or in dysfunctional set ups, with various staff, neighbours or friends, being relied upon to bring the child up. Any set up that results in inconsistencies or neglect for significant periods of time during the formative years. Many, I believe, also have a narcissistic parent and so this is modelled to the child in a number of deep-seating ways. Any child of a narcissistic parent will likely be watching and learning a variety of unhealthy and manipulative ways of being in order to get needs met. They won't have much chance of learning healthy boundaries, responsibility or learning empathy. This also has a huge impact on the ability to relate to people and form relationships.

Narcissistic adults I meet and hear about in my work tend to have experienced early developmental damage, whether it be related to abandonment, neglect or some significant disruption in early relationships. It's important to highlight that children also do not need the absolute 'perfect' childhood in order to thrive. Healthy emotional development relies on having early needs met, just enough to support emotional development. In particular this also includes supporting the learning of recognising that actions have consequences. This helps to develop a sense of personal responsibility – something narcissists have not learnt. With narcissists, the early experiences usually equate to quite significant forms of emotional neglect or abuse. Some examples of the early experiences relating to narcissism include:

Rob recognised narcissistic personality traits and this had been pointed out to him during rehab for alcoholism. A successful businessman, he had struggled with addictions most of his life; alcohol, drugs, gambling and sex. Whilst he managed to sustain abstinence from alcohol and drugs, his addictive and narcissistic behaviours were active with ongoing issues around sex and love addiction and gambling. He would oscillate between defensiveness and denial around his addictive behaviours, becoming quickly arrogant or aggressive and yet at times, be able to seemingly genuinely recognise his issues. His earlier life had been traumatic. His mother was an alcoholic, his father was unknown. During the early years of his life, his mother was preoccupied with her own alcoholism, depression and relationship issues, repeatedly falling for the 'wrong' men. She experienced violence from partners, Rob witnessed this as a youngster. Through her drinking, she would leave him for long periods of time and his physical and emotional needs were neglected. At the age of 4 years old, Rob was sent to live with an Aunt who then also did not care for him properly. He would often be left hungry and uncared for. By the time he was 8 years old he had been placed into care. By this point, his narcissistic defences are already developed in response to such significant and early neglect and abuse. The lack of any consistent support, healthy mirroring, unconditional love and regard, would have by then, already caused enough damage that a range of narcissistic defence mechanisms are developed in order to keep him away from connecting with the psychological and emotional pain. An over focus then on drive and over-achievement is then adopted in a bid to keep feelings of shame and worthlessness at bay. That is often the driving force behind work addiction and over-achieving.

Lucy was an only child born to strict, authoritarian career and achievement-focused parents. They had rigid, although at times inconsistent parenting, as they would alternate between being very doting, over-indulgent parents when they had the time and energy, to being quite harsh disciplinarians with rigid rules and boundaries. Quite a confusing picture for any child to grow up in. As a result, Lucy adopted a range of manipulative ways in which to behave with each parent, in order to get her way. As her parents were focused on their careers largely, offering consistent health boundaries was, they felt, too difficult and thus Lucy learnt to manipulate, to push and effectively bully her way to get whatever she wanted. This continued and developed throughout her school life. Whilst arrogant and haughty, she also experienced self-doubt and issues with self-esteem. She became increasingly controlling and would flip out into rages to get her own way as a child and teenager. She actually couldn't control the emotional anguish of not having things how she demanded. During her late teens she become increasingly rigid and controlled around her eating and developed anorexia nervosa. For many years she denied this and even though she sought help from mental health services, she would lie and try to manipulate staff. She came across as arrogant, dismissive, belittling and rude.

Mark was the youngest of four children. His parents were young. They were inexperienced, with very little support from their families. However, they were determined. They had stuck together and were hard-workers. In hindsight, after Mark was born, his mother had struggled with post-natal depression. Sadly, this was at a time when this debilitating condition was not so recognised or understood. His mother struggled on, becoming less active, spending periods of time in bed, crying whilst the family had the harsh view of "toughen up" and "get on with it". She struggled considerably. This interfered quite significantly with the formation of a bond between her and her son. Her husband tried hard to support the family however had his own struggles with trying to care for four children, largely without any other support. Mark felt different from the family and would become very angry as a toddler and young child, frequently getting into trouble for being aggressive. In time, and with the help of a very supportive teacher, Mark actually learnt to focus his energies on his studies and became highly driven and a very high achiever. As an adult he was a highly determined and successful entrepreneur, making huge amounts of money and enjoying all that came with his self-made wealth. He was rarely happy though, he suffered with ongoing depression and anxiety but was reluctant to seek help for it as he was paranoid about anybody finding out or anybody thinking badly of him. Instead he maintained a work addiction, fuelled by an egotistical drive to acquire materialistic possessions in a bid to feel better about himself. This only ever served a very short-lived high before he would 'need' more, nothing was ever enough for him. He had many failed superficial relationships and regularly used sex workers. Nothing could satisfy him or his longings.

If you've ever experienced a narcissist in full flow or in a narcissistic rage, you have probably seen in essence the little toddler in them. Watching a narcissist in a narcissistic rage is like watching a toddler tantrum in action complete with screaming, shouting and trying all manner of weird and wonderful ways to manipulate and get what they want, including the throwing of toys out of the pram and all around the place! Narcissists essentially revert to the very young child (usually under the age of four or five years old) where they are attempting to win the attention and approval they so desperately need in whichever way they can.

There has been some quite significant changes in parental trends over the last few years. As previously mentioned, narcissists tend to experience quite early neglect or abuse in one form or another and this kind of emotional stunt in early development certainly is associated with adult narcissistic personality disorder.

Parenting and the development
of narcissistic personality

Two main types of childhood experience seem to associate with narcissistic personality disorder. They are extreme and complete opposite in nature. The first is the sort of emotional neglect or abuse already outlined. The other, is something that I think we are just beginning to see more and more of in recent years – that being extreme overindulgence in our children. The over-the-top parenting that involves a continual gushing of how the child is utterly amazing and brilliant at everything. That every piece of unintelligible art work completed at nursery is an absolute masterpiece, encouraging the child's belief that they can do no wrong, can walk on water and are perfect is arguably equally as unhealthy for their development. In any case, extremes of anything are rarely healthy. The healthy ground is somewhere in between, complete with rupture and repair, as well as all the mistakes and learning along the way.

Research in this area suggests that the following parental influences and experience during childhood are possibly linked to the development of Narcissistic Personality Disorder:

* Severe emotional abuse or neglect in early childhood.
* Erratic / unpredictable / unreliable caregiving from parents.
* Excessive admiration and lack of balanced, realistic feedback.
* Extreme / excessive praise for good behaviours or extreme / excessive criticism for perceived bad behaviours.
* Overindulgence by parents, peers or other family members.
* Valued by parents as a means to regulate their own self-esteem.
* Learning ways to manipulate from parents or peers. ie. Narcissism modelled or learnt from narcissistic parent.

(Groopman, & Cooper, 2006)

NARCISSISM IN THERAPY

Because narcissism is often related to very early emotional and psychological damage, it is therefore very difficult to treat. In fact, narcissistic personality disorder is regarded as one of the most difficult psychiatric conditions to work with. If not for any other reason than because a true narcissist is the least likely person to seek out or enter therapy or treatment. If they do it is usually because it serves as a function to manipulate something from someone else. If they do attend therapy, they will usually sit and complain about how it's everybody else fault and they will more than likely portray to the therapist about how they are the victim and are misunderstood. They are the personality types that will likely replicate narcissistic abuse within the therapeutic relationship. This often begins with attempts to impress and seduce the therapist by, for example, showering with compliments or gifts, eg. making bold statements such as *"you're the best therapist I've ever seen"*, *"you're the only one that really understands me"*, or by boasting about who they know, how much money they have, or attempt to come across like the 'perfect client' – all in order to seek and obtain the therapists approval or admiration. They struggle to accept personal responsibility and with little or no capacity for honest self-reflection will likely struggle to truly engage in the therapy. Therapy is challenging at the best of times. As in many relationships with a narcissist, if or when challenged or not held in high enough esteem, the narcissist will simply cut ties at the drop of a hat and abruptly end therapy. Leaving with the belief that the therapy wasn't helpful at all and the issues and failure lies entirely with the therapist. Narcissists will use 'going to therapy' as a means to indirectly manipulate or guilt-trip their partner or other relationships or institutions. Attending therapy once or even several times a week is quite different to actively engaging in therapy.

Reflection point:

It can be helpful in making sense of the origins of a narcissistic personality to understand more about the early life and family background of others. This in itself can be informative for your own understanding. What do you know about the early life experiences of your current / ex partner / narcissist in your life? Does some of this relate?

Remember this is just for your own understanding. This is not about feeling sorry for or responsible for the narcissists experience or being pulled into fixing or rescuing. This is about your own recovery process.

4.   What is Narcissistic Abuse?

Narcissism in essence, is a defence against deep and intense feelings of shame. Shame is an awful feeling. Shame is the feeling that tells us that we are defected, useless, worthless and unlovable. For a narcissist, it is simply too psychologically unbearable to connect with this shame and deep inner pain. Their psychology and actions therefore seek to defend them from doing so. It would simply be too much for their mind and fragile ego state to cope with. In their ongoing bid to keep well away from this deep pain and damage, narcissists rely on a variety of mental and psychological defence mechanisms and destructive behaviours. Much of these actions, when it is focused on those around them, are abusive. Abuse can be emotional, psychological, physical, sexual, financial or spiritual.

Abuse of any kind is abuse. It is <u>never</u> acceptable.

Narcissistic abuse is also often referred to as 'invisible abuse'. Unlike physical abuse where the results are clear and undebatable in the form of bruises or cuts, narcissistic abuse and bullying is often seemingly very subtle, especially in the beginning. It is usually progressive and at times very difficult for people to spot. Narcissistic abuse is often executed in a way where nobody else, aside from the victim, sees or suspects it. In fact, often narcissistic abuse is so manipulative and abusive that often sufferers are left unsure if what they are experiencing is abuse at all. Instead, many people end up feeling - because they are told such by the narcissist - that they are simply being too sensitive, that they're overreacting, imagining things, or that it's them and their fault. A key feature of narcissistic and related emotional abuse is by the means of the abuser, then saying it's you and your fault, that you are the one to blame. As a result of this kind of abuse, it's very typical that you then deny or doubt your own perception. That in itself is a fundamental sign of narcissistic abuse.

Other indicators and characteristics of narcissistic abuse include:

Boundary violation: Narcissists have no boundaries. They also have very little, if any, respect for anybody else's space or personal belongings. Boundaries can be physical, sexual, mental or emotional and are vital for healthy relationships. For a narcissist, their wants or needs are always the priority. Even if they may pretend otherwise, it is usually with the aim of ultimately getting what they want.

Denial: A point blank inability to accept or acknowledge any truth, responsibility or error. The level of denial and absolute assurance that often accompanies it in a narcissist can be quite alarming. (I have met narcissists that would quite adamantly deny the sky is blue on a bright summers day!)

Devaluation: in opposed to idealisation, devaluation relates to highlighting or pointing out other peoples faults of flaws in order to knock the other person and basically to help them to feel better about themselves.

Divide & Conquer: Often through idealisation or devaluing or indeed any other forms of manipulation, a narcissist will try to split people apart in groups, in family or at work. This gives them a sense of power. Divide & conquer describes the split and alienation the narcissist with create in a chosen individual who will then be set apart from the others – either in a positive 'chosen' capacity or through alienation and bullying. This serves to weaken and isolate group members. It often leads to fall outs within the group, as well as paranoia, mistrust, resentments and competition, essentially leaving it easier for the narcissist to maintain control in the dynamic.

Emotional Blackmail: This includes anything that is communicated to you that is experienced as threatening or intimidating. This also includes punishment, silent treatment, use of anger, aggression or threats. Emotional blackmail is intended to elicit feelings of fear, guilt and compliance. A narcissist will simply use emotional blackmail in order to get what they want. They have little, if any regard for the welfare or affect that has on you. They will often deny they are even doing it. Or they will use other techniques to turn things back on you repeatedly, perhaps suggesting you are exaggerating or being 'too sensitive'.

Exploitation: Taking advantage and using people to serve their own gains and ambitions. A narcissist will not think twice about doing this. For them it is second nature.

Finger pointing: A narcissist will never genuinely take responsibility for themselves. They never or rarely apologise – they will not feel the need to. They will instead attempt to keep any accusations, blame or responsibility away from them by pointing out what anybody and everybody else is doing or not doing. In any argument or dispute, a narcissist will be highly skilled at turning the focus onto somebody else and making others feel like they are the ones at fault. They keep the heat off themselves by constantly pointing fingers at other peoples actions, words or behaviours.

Fishing: This is when the narcissist, just like a fisherman, will throw out 'hooks' in order to catch their supper. They will be attuned into using the exact bait necessary to catch and reel their target in. It can be very helpful to identify for yourself what kinds of bait leaves you vulnerable. What have been the hooks that have pulled you back in before? For example, is it your feelings of guilt, their use of fear or anxiety-inducing comments or behaviours? A need to rescue or fix within you? It can be helpful to work to identify your vulnerable bait or pulls. Awareness is a first step to change.

Gas-lighting: Gas-Lighting is a term used to describe how a narcissist will say and do things that will leave you second guessing yourself, doubting your own reality, your own judgements or perceptions. It is highly psychologically abusive and dangerous. Through gas-lighting, you begin to doubt yourself, lose trust in yourself and as a result, at times feel like you are losing your mind. In extreme cases, it can lead to having a complete nervous breakdown.

Ghosting: Narcissists do not manage endings. Ghosting is when they end a relationship by suddenly cutting ties and all communication without any discussion or explanation. The shock of this can be traumatising.

Idealisation: the worshipping or an individual or organisation. Narcissists and many people with personality issues tend to view things in extremes – either good or bad, black and white. With idealisation a person or thing is viewed as incredible, the best thing since sliced bread, perfection. Is it also this kind of validation they seek from others. Parents of narcissists also either tend to completely worship their child in this way, as if the child can walk on water, or relate in the other extreme, where they are devalued and not good enough.

Inconsistencies: The one thing you can rely on with many narcissists is that they are consistent in their inconsistencies. Be it with words and/or behaviours. Saying one thing and doing something else that is completely at odds with that. eg. declaring they want to be with you, but not acting like it, or being unable to commit, despite promises of commitment.

Isolation: An abuser of any kind will ultimately be aiming to isolate their victim away from friends, family or colleagues. People are more vulnerable and easier to manipulate, control and abuse when isolated. Narcissists aim to achieve this in a variety of ways including trying to be seen to have your best interests at heart, For example, *'those friends are no good for you, you are better than that'* or perhaps insisting you give up work, that they'd take care of things financially (financial control). Through negative judgements, gas-lighting and manipulation, slowly but surely, they will aim to isolate you away from loved ones and create an over-reliance on them.

Judging: A defence mechanism commonly seen in narcissists where they will comment negatively and harshly on other peoples actions, choices, speech, looks, abilities and so on. Passing judgement on others serves to make them feel better about themselves and also helps them to maintain a position of superiority.

Love-bombing: Overwhelming others with affection and attention, compliments, praise and gifts in order to gain their interest and 'love'. The aim of love-bombing is ultimately to manipulate and control.

Lying: Standard for any narcissist. This can be anything from slight exaggerations of the truth to out and out complete and utter fabrications, creation of false identities and point blank denial.

Projecting: The suggestion or accusation that you are the one with their issues. They will accuse you of the very behaviours or feeling states they are exhibiting or experiencing. *'You're being paranoid/over-sensitive'. 'You are so selfish!', 'You are acting like you've got something to hide...'* even *'You're a narcissist!'.*

Responsibility: Not taking any. For a narcissist, it is very typical they will have zero ability to take personal responsibility. It is invariably always yours and everybody else's fault/issue/responsibility. They will want to convince both themselves and others that they are the victim. *'I cheated because you weren't there... if you were there for me then I wouldn't have had to sleep with anybody else!'* People cheat because they want to. It is their choice and their responsibility.

Slander: Spreading lies and rumours to cause harm and damage. Also to illicit a sense of power and control.

Toddler Tantrums – Underneath the arrogant exterior lies an emotionally stunted child (usually within the first 4 or 5 years of life). They have little ability to operate as a grown up emotionally and so will react in very childish ways, effectively throwing their toys out of their pram, shouting, screaming, storming off, giving you the silent treatment and other forms of emotional manipulation. In a bid to feel better about themselves they will often judge or belittle others, be scathing or otherwise cruel and hostile. They will want to devalue others to feel better about themselves or to ease the deep inner turmoil they experience and have no emotional skills to deal with.

Topping: Most narcissists have a habit of 'topping' or 'upping' above anything anybody else has achieved, obtained or owns. This serves to quickly return the focus of attention and admiration to them. Narcissists find it difficult to tolerate enjoying the success or achievements of others. Topping can also include negative bragging about such things as illness. For example, if you have a health concern, such as a headache, they already have a brain tumour. Topping fuels competitiveness and cheating.

Verbal Abuse: This can be done through a range from subtle (snidey, ambiguous, indirect comments) to blatant direct abuse (shouting/screaming). Other types of verbal abuse include: name calling, belittling, shaming, blaming, demanding, manipulating, sarcasm, criticising, judging, undermining, interrupting / not letting the other person speak, not listening, laughing. Silent treatment is also a form of verbal abuse.

Withholding: Narcissists need to feel power and control. Withholding offers them this sense. They gain a sense of control and power by holding back and controlling money, communication, affections, etc.

Violence: Physical abuse, hitting, pushing, shoving, pulling hair, slapping, restraining, throwing or damaging you or your belongings. Narcissists can be violent, however in my experience I consider it to be more common that narcissistic abuse is done in a more sophisticated, discreet and hidden manner than that. They are more likely to not want to leave any physical evidence or marks that can clearly identify their actions, preferring instead more subtle forms that they can more easily deny.

IDENTIFYING NARCISSISTIC ABUSE

Narcissistic abuse can be tricky to identify at first, especially when you are in the midst of it. Being in a relationship with a narcissist and experiencing any one of the above specific forms of abuse is often highly confusing and destabilising. It is highly psychologically and emotionally abusive. That is the aim from a narcissists perspective. When we are caught off guard, when we are shocked or confused, we are more vulnerable to being manipulated. It is very difficult to think with clarity or to see the situation with any clear perspective. Another reason why it can be so hard to identify narcissistic abuse is because of how good things appear in the early days. The early stages of meeting and dating a narcissist are often like a dream... before it turns into a nightmare. Some times it can even feel too good to be true. If things feel too good to be true, it's usually because they are. That in itself is a warning sign all too often we do not recognise or want to accept at the time.

A narcissist will be looking to partner with somebody who can meet their narcissistic supply needs. In other words, somebody who has an appealing status or are able to offer them enough consistent admiration, adoration and attention, financial or status gains. This is often achieved by the narcissists 'love-bombing' in the early stages of meeting or dating. Love-bombing creates an intensity that can be absolutely blinding, mesmerising and paralysing. When the beginnings of this abuse begins, usually within the first few months, many people are, by that stage, so high on the intensity of the 'love' that they fail to recognise the warning signs. Or perhaps, in part, do not see the reality because of their own fantasies around relationships. Many people do not want to accept or consider the reality of the situation. They will deny the warning signs in the hope and fantasy that things are or will be fine. Either way, it's easy to miss warning signs at the time due to the stark contrast in perceived behaviours. It is important to remember though, **intensity is not the same as intimacy.** Don't get the two confused.

When the beginnings of the noticeable abuse appears we simply cannot fathom how somebody can be so wonderful and kind one moment, and then so awful and vitriolic the next. The shock of this transition can leave us doubting that this is even happening... *"perhaps I am imagining things, or getting it wrong?"* On some level, we can also become stuck at that initial love-bombing phase. It can be so overwhelming and intense that we are left unable to register any deviation from that and then the weeks, months and years go by. In some sense, it can pull the partner into an obsessive addiction, where they are desperate to hold onto or recreate that initial or occasional high. I see clients who are still holding onto the hope that their narcissistic partner will change decades into abuse. People become addicted to the fantasy of how they might imagine things to be, or a fantasy of what they would like. These things obscure the view of reality. A distorted view of reality in itself indicates an unhealthy and potentially damaging relationship. The path out of this and to the road of recovery involves a number of key fundamentals. The first is becoming more grounded and realistic, moving away from fantasy or idealistic thinking to a perspective that is more grounded in reality, objective, present and helpful. Other key factors for recovery include working on your own stuff; your self-esteem, self-worth, self-care, compassion and forgiveness, communication and boundaries. All of these and more are covered in the following chapters.

Reflection point:

* What specific forms of narcissistic abuse do you recognise in the person/people you have in mind?
* Do any specific memories or examples of this come to mind?
* How did you feel at the time? How did you react? What happened?
* What do you think and how do you feel about this now?
* What do you need in order to take good care of myself right now? What would you like? What can you do to attend to your own self-care needs today?

5.   Relational Dynamics – The Drama Triangle

The 'Drama triangle' is a model of destructive social interaction and conflict originally proposed by Stephen Karpman in the late 1960s. It is a model used mostly in transactional analysis to illustrate and map out drama and conflict intense relationship interactions (Karpman, 2014). This drama triangle is a dynamic often seen with narcissists and is what relentlessly plays out in relationships of narcissistic abuse. Please see Karpmans website and book for further information (listed in references at end of book).

The three positions within Karpmans drama triangle are the Victim, the Persecutor and the Rescuer.

The Victim: The 'victim' position is the "poor me" stance. The person in this position sees themselves as being victimised, bullied, being hard done by, helpless, hopeless, persecuted or oppressed. Being a 'victim' is used to maintain a helpless position and they are therefore unlikely or unmotivated to take any responsibility for their actions or the situation. There are essentially gains to be made by holding a victim position – there is somebody else to blame and there is usually somebody else that is willing to come to the rescue.

The Persecutor: The persecutor is the bully on the attack. In this case, the classic narcissist. In the case of the narcissist, this is the position of blaming, shaming, controlling, being aggressive, oppressive, judgemental or authoritative, threatening and/or arrogant. A narcissist usually targets an individual or institution to blame or criticise.

The Rescuer: The rescuer is often the classic codependent, echoist, enabler, people-pleaser, fixer and/or helper. The rescuer responds to the real or portrayed 'helplessness' of the victim. The person in the rescue position will assume responsibility on the 'victims' behalf. This is an over-responsibility. The rescuer will take on responsibility for situations or issues that are not theirs. Often the rescuer to the narcissist is driven to rescue due to their own anxieties, fears or feelings of guilt. The rescuer, by the very action of rescuing, prevents the victim from taking responsibility for themselves. Rescuing is a key part in maintaining unhealthy and toxic relationship dynamics.

The narcissist shifts quite skilfully between any one of these positions although most commonly is found assuming the role of the persecutor or the victim. They can though also use the position of rescuer to control and manipulate. By shifting into any one of the three positions, the narcissist by doing so, then begins the drama triangle dynamic. They then seek to 'pull' others into the remaining positions, to join and complete the drama triangle thus creating drama, conflict, addictive and toxic relationship dynamics and patterns. Once pulled into a drama triangle, people can move between the different roles in varied situations, however the ongoing movement between positions maintains the drama, conflict and unhealthy relationships.

For example, the narcissist may start with placing themselves in 'victim' role by telling others how badly a certain person or organisation has treated them. They will explain and tell stories about how the person or organisation has treated them unfairly, have been inappropriate, unprofessional, controlling or aggressive and in various ways, paint the 'other' out as the terrible and unfair persecutor or bully. In reality, this may or may not have any truth to it. By putting themselves in the victim position and stating all about how others have been so bad to them (usually without acknowledging any part or responsibility of their own in it) they seek then to pull a 'rescuer' and sympathiser into the mix to commence the drama triangle. The helplessness or upset of the 'victim' can pull on the heart strings or caring nature of the partner and friend who then step in attempt to rescue, fix, appease or care-take.

"My girlfriend would often be talking about fall-outs with people she's had at work, especially coming into conflict with her bosses. In the first five years of our relationship, she had four different jobs, all coming to an end for the same reasons – serious fall outs and disagreements with her boss and colleagues. One had even ended in a bitter legal dispute. Every time, she had been the person who had been wronged. She had been mistreated and treated unfairly by colleagues. It was someone else's fault, every time. It was only when I was talking to my therapist about the latest work-related conflict that they pointed out this pattern. I realised that every time, whenever I listened to her complaining about how terrible her colleagues had treated her, she was playing the victim. She never ever looked at her part in the difficulties (much like in our relationship) and instead just blamed everyone else and be like "poor me". Every time I would empathise with her and feel her upset. I felt awful for her and would try to comfort her or try to find practical solutions to help the situation. Whenever

I did though, she would turn on me and start attacking me for not helping in the right way. Nothing I could do or suggest was good enough. It was awful. I was constantly pulled into feeling sorry for her, even strangely feeling responsible for her, like it was my fault or my problem to sort out. I guess nobody likes to see a loved one in pain but the fact this was a repeating pattern made me realise that there was a common denominator in the mix – her!

Even so, whenever I tried to help I was made to feel useless. Like I'd made the worse suggestions ever, didn't understand or was stupid. In the end I didn't know what to do anymore – nothing was 'right'. It was only when I started to speak to the counsellor about this, that I started to understand the drama triangle and how she would go from victim to persecutor in a second, whilst I was left anxiously trying to make it all better. The more I started to recognise this, the more I was able to resist getting pulled in. I started to see that this was her problem, and she was a part of it, and so it was her responsibility to do something about it. Not that she would. She would just move on and in the end not speak to me about it any longer. She found other people she could pull into the drama. I was punished and blamed for not being understanding or good enough to be involved. In the end I was pleased about this. I was able to recognise her doing this in her work situation. It was like a light went off in my head and I could see how this is exactly what she did in our relationship. Always making out like things were my fault or my responsibility. We have now recently separated and whilst it is hard in many ways, I actually do feel so much better. I am certainly feeling better about myself and more confident. I feel clearer about what is my responsibility and what is not. I've actually realised I am a man who just enjoys a simple, straightforward life. All that drama was exhausting and relentless. I'm so glad I'm away from it now. I can relax. I even sleep better now."

The ongoing drama, conflict or abuse with a narcissist ends when one person – YOU – decide to leave the triangle. And choose to not re-enter the drama. Recognising this triangle playing out in action can help with your awareness of this as it happens. The more you recognise the signs and characteristics of each position, as well as any pull *within you* to move into a position, the easier it will be to then resist automatically being drawn in. Mindful awareness and self-care is key. It also helps to make a commitment to yourself, if you want to end the madness of narcissistic abuse, to work to recognise the drama triangle in action and the various positions. Being aware can create a space in which you can then resist being pulled in.

Reflection point:

* What do you recognise from the Drama Triangle model in your own dynamic?
* What positions do you recognise?
* What position do you feel you most often get pulled into?
* How might you recognise this in the future?
* What is happening in you prior to or when you step into position? This may be a part of what is triggered in you that then propels you into a role? Anxiety? Guilt? A sense of responsibility? Anything else?
* What might help stop you from getting involved in the drama triangle?

6. Fantasy vs Reality – Keeping it real

One of the dangerous traps that is very easy to find yourself trapped in with a narcissist is one of *elusive fantasy*. Many people who find themselves in romantic relationships with narcissists can remain stuck in destructive and unhealthy relationships for long periods of time. One of the reasons for this is because they are spending more time living in fantasy land than they are grounded in reality. Fantasy land is where it is all too easy to believe the lies a narcissist will tell you. It is where you justify the narcissists actions, downplay it, pretend to others and yourself that *'things aren't so bad'*. In fantasy we desperately cling onto the dream and hope that one day the narcissist will change... that things will be different. It is understandable to see why it can be hard to let go of the latter hope when it comes to a narcissist. Usually they have overwhelmingly love-bombed in the early stages and first impressions tend to last. The early stages of an abusive relationship can be absolutely wonderful, exciting and exhilarating – it's a high. More often than not, a narcissist has gotten close to us at a time of vulnerability. They have appeared to rescue. We've become dependent – or so we believe. Either way, a narcissist will make all manner of wonderful promises and set up all kinds of expectations. Then things start to change, and slowly but surely the subtle and sometimes not so subtle abuse begins. Abuse is often followed by another round of love-bombing, romance or wonder-overwhelm and then you can find yourself pulled back into the fantasy trap. Months, years or even decades of increasing narcissistic abuse, betrayals, lies, broken promises and trauma... partners can still find themselves hanging on for the day when he/she will be nice and wonderful, sweet, romantic and considerate again. *"Like he/she was at the beginning"*. It's as if our brains cannot update to the present moment and the present reality.

Echoist, codependent or love-addicted partners are desperate to hold onto the elusive hope and dream that things may change. That the narcissist will do what they say. Even though they might accept that the narcissists behaviours are abusive or inappropriate, the dangerous fantasy and arguably narcissistic belief is that *they* can be the ones to change them. Perhaps because; *"I'm the only one that truly understands him"*, *"I can see the 'real' her – she only shows that side to me"*. *"I see their vulnerability"*, *"we have such a deep connection"*, *"nobody can love them or know them like I can (or vice versa)"*, *"they said things will be different"*. This is fantasy talk and a key ingredient for an unhealthy, destructive relationship. There is also an element of narcissism in these kinds of beliefs. It can be somewhat of a martyrdom notion in believing you effectively have special powers that enable you to change somebody else's deep-seated issues and life-long ways of being. You can't. And in addition, it is not your responsibility to fix or help them either. Why would you even want to?

I would like to share with you as a qualified and experienced psychologist that narcissistic personality is one of *the* most difficult clinical issues to work with and address. It is a very tall order for highly trained and qualified clinical practitioners to address and even then it is only possible if the client is highly motivated, committed and willing and able for positive change. It is very difficult – so the rest of us surely have a lesser chance of miraculously being able to heal the narcissistic wounds in others. More to the point, *why would you want to?* (This is an important question to reflect on as this reflects more about you, not them).

In healthy, emotionally mature relationships, adults take responsibility for themselves as well as for their own actions and choices. Narcissists and codependent partners may tend to argue that *'he/she made me do it"*, *"you made me feel like this"* and *"if you didn't behave in such a way then I wouldn't have to get angry/lie/cheat etc."* Blaming others and believing that other people are completely responsible for your wellbeing and personal choices or similarly, that you are responsible for anybody else's mood or behaviour is unhealthy and dysfunctional. It is fantasy nonsense. Don't get me wrong here... yes, of course what we do and say will have an impact on others to some extent. Yes, we of course will be affected to some extent by other people, their words and their actions. We are not robots. However, we are then responsible for what *we do next* and how we hold and maintain *our own* personal boundaries. Ultimately you are responsible for your own happiness, your own wellbeing and your personal choices.

It is damaging and in extreme cases life-threatening to continue putting up with increasingly abusive or detrimental behaviour. Often in abusive relationships, especially of this kind, the undermining and cruelty is subtle and develops slowly in a way that becomes hard to detect. This together with gas-lighting tactics can trigger partners into doubting their own experience and deciding that perhaps certain abuse didn't even happen. We wonder if perhaps we have over interpreted, imagined things or overreacted. A narcissist will happily be the first to suggest you are being *"too sensitive"*. Cue being back to *"It's me and my fault"*. Usually, in narcissistic abusive, partners are already feeling to blame anyway as self-esteem and confidence has been chipped away by the relationship.

Not all narcissists are the overt, charismatic and gregarious kind. The power/fame/success hungry egotists and their clear selfish, self-seeking behaviours are easier to spot than the more subtle and sophisticated charms of the covert narcissist. It is important to familiarise yourself with the fundamental traits of a narcissist such as their inability to take responsibility for themselves, the habitual way they will turn blame on you, that it is all about them, the use of various forms of manipulation in order to get what they want, the need to appear or feel better, special or different to others, being judgemental and so on. Either way, in making important, albeit, difficult steps to recognise narcissistic abuse it is vital you are able to take stock and assess your experiences in an honest and objective manner. This is not always the most comfortable or enjoyable thing to do, however it is vital in order to regain a more balanced perspective. It is an essential step in recovery to start to spend more and more time grounded in reality. You need to connect to the present-day reality and spend less time in fantasy and hope – however painful that may be at times.

I personally believe in and advocate the power of writing and putting pen to paper. Seeing your own personal experience in black and white can help you develop a more objective, realistic and balanced perspective to what's going on. I recommend writing a diary or journaling. Please get started if you aren't already doing this. It can be helpful in so many ways to begin to put your thoughts, feelings and experiences down on paper. It can help you to process and make sense of what's happened. It can be cathartic and cleansing. It may also help you to discover and express your emotional experience, be it anger, grief, frustration, confusion, fears or otherwise. It can help you take more of an objective stock on your relationship. You may find it helpful to write in a systematic inventory way. The following questions are designed to help with taking an honest appraisal of specific incidences and experiences. However if you find you prefer to just write freely, then by all means do that. Whatever it is that works for you.

QUESTIONS TO ASK YOURSELF ABOUT YOUR EXPERIENCE:

1. What happened?
2. What was the worst part?
3. What did he/she/they do?
4. What did I do?
5. How did I feel?
6. What were my automatic thoughts or beliefs about myself or the situation?
7. What would I say to a loved on if they were telling me this had happened to them? What would family or good friends say about this?
8. Is there anything I need to do? What do I need that I can offer myself right now?

Reflection points:

* Have I had fantasy thinking about this relationship / situation?
* What are/were the fantasy and hopes specifically?
* What happened?
* What are the things that happen, that is said or done or the feelings that I have that seem to trigger me into fantasy or elusive hope?
* What pulls me into fantasy thinking, beliefs or hopes?
* Why? What happens?
* Do I recognise any pattern to this at all?
* Take a balanced perspective. A narcissist will not change.
* How can I better take care of myself if/when I feel like this again?

7.

Your secret weapon – Arm yourself with information

Something that I believe is an important and necessary part of the recovery process is arming yourself with as much information as possible about narcissism and narcissistic abuse.

KNOWLEDGE IS POWER

Thankfully, over recent years, there has been a huge increase in general public awareness of narcissism and narcissistic abuse. This is a really helpful step in increasing awareness of this in our society and learning to recognise this in relationships, in the work place, families and elsewhere. With awareness comes change. It becomes easier to spot the signs – a fundamental step in recovery. With being able to spot the signs you can arm yourself with awareness and crucially avoid becoming involved with raging narcissists again in the future.

I have witnessed a real shift in my private practice over recent years in regard to this awareness. Just a few years ago I would often meet clients for the first time coming to therapy complaining of feeling like they were going crazy. They arrived in the hope of learning how to change themselves in some way, or be a 'better' person, a better partner, a better son or daughter, or a better employee, all in order to win the approval, gain peace or acknowledgement, regard or love from their narcissistic *partner/ parent/boss. Many people seek therapy for support in working out what is wrong with *them*. They would complain of a sense of never really feeling 'enough' and that anything they did was not good enough. This is often a key identifier of what it feels like to be in relationship with a narcissist. Issues in a relationship are not down to one person. If it is a relationship issue, then that means there is at least two people involved! If the other person in the relationship is a narcissist, then they will likely make you feel like it *is* all your 'fault' and your responsibility. This is a part of what narcissistic abuse is. Partners of narcissists end up feeling less than, not good enough and like nothing you do will ever be good enough.

Just a few years back, often clients I worked with had never heard the term narcissist or narcissistic abuse. They were convinced it was them and that they were the problem. Usually the narcissist in their lives had openly suggested and encouraged this idea. I want to be clear here, that any relationship issue, by the very nature of *relationship* involves more than one person. Therefore more than one person has a part and has a responsibility to how that relationship functions. One of the difficulties with being in a relationship with a narcissist is that they are unwilling and unable to take responsibility for themselves. Hence why one of the narcissists favourite mottos is *"It's you and your fault"* ,*"You're to blame"* and *"It's your responsibility"*. This notion is childish, nonsense and quite simply narcissistic. Considering that the issues lay within the relationship dynamic, rather than solely one person is a new concept for many people to accept. Although encouragingly, I see more and more clients arriving for therapy already wondering… *"Is this narcissistic abuse…?"*, *"I think my partner is a narcissist"*, *"I think my boss is a narcissist"*. or *"Was mum narcissistic?"*.

It is really encouraging to see terms and a broader understanding of narcissistic and unseen/invisible abuse being more openly discussed in the mainstream. Such awareness and the increase of information available online, in books, magazines etc. being more on our radar truly helps us to be more conscious and vigilant – for ourselves and our friends, family and loved ones. I cannot recommend enough that you arm yourself with as much information as possible around this subject. Particularly at the early stages of recognising or starting to come to terms with your own experience of narcissistic abuse. Read books, blogs, forums, watch videos, talk to others who may understand or already have had similar experiences. It can be helpful to understand more about narcissism and help make some sense of your own experience. Learning about narcissistic abuse often helps people to start to recognise that it is not them. It's the narcissist and it's narcissistic abuse. This is an important realisation at the early stages of recovery.

In short, for now and for this chapter, I wanted to just offer a further overview of the sorts of things I would see in clients coming to see me whether they were already aware they were experiencing narcissistic abuse or not. Generally speaking, many people seeking therapy who are experiencing narcissistic abuse struggle, to varying degrees, with low self-esteem, low self-worth, confidence issues and often demonstrate self doubt – despite paradoxically often being very driven, highly accomplished and successful. They are often highly stressed, on the verge of burn-out, anxious or panicky. Many people feel confused about why they are struggling and that can be a frightening place to be.

Some other common experiences include:

* Sense of confusion – (about the relationship, their judgement and take on things…)
* Low self-esteem

* A strong sense of *"I'm not good enough"* or of not being *"enough"*
* Self doubt
* Distressing loss of sense of self *"I don't know who I am anymore"*
* Panic attacks / anxiety
* Depression / hopelessness
* Symptoms of trauma / PTSD
* Difficulties with eating over-eating/under-eating
* Sleep problems, waking up suddenly in the night or inability to sleep / over-sleeping
* Nervousness
* Paranoia
* Obsessive-compulsive symptoms or behaviours / rituals
* Isolation / lack of social support / feeling like friends or colleagues don't understand or see it
* Feelings of guilt and shame
* Fatigue
* Denial
* No or little sense of personal boundaries / unable to say 'no'
* Often some inclusion of physical health problems related to stress, eg. IBS, aches and pain, skin problems, autoimmune disorders
* Stress & Burnout
* Suicidal thoughts and feelings
* In extreme cases being on the verge or in complete burn-out or nervous breakdown.

Common complaints I hear patients express in the first or early sessions if they've recently experienced or are experiencing narcissistic abuse include:

* "I feel like I'm going mad"
* "It's me, it's my fault"

* "Nothing I do is enough"
* "I'm the problem"
* "I can't cope"
* "I don't know what's going on"
* "I'm not good enough"
* "Is it me or them?"
* "I feel lost"
* "I don't know who I am anymore..."
* "I'm a bag of nerves"
* "I can't trust my own judgement"
* "I feel guilty"
* "It's something I can / should fix (ie. It's my responsibility)"
* "If only I could.... (then he/she/the relationship would be OK)"
* "It's down to me"

"It was actually Jane that kept telling me I should go and speak to somebody in the first place. I believed I was doing right by her. I was working hard, taking care of things, paying all the bills, even giving her an allowance to live on each month. I'd book holidays, buy her things, but nothing was ever enough for her. She would put me under pressure and be constantly telling me about what friends or neighbours had got. If somebody had a new TV, we would need to have an even bigger, better one. I just went along with much of it to keep the peace. I wanted to make her happy – that was important to me. When she wasn't I felt bad. I felt guilty and like it was my fault or my responsibility. We argued a lot and over the smallest of things. Things would get so blown out of proportion and there were times when I felt so bamboozled by her hysterics and rage that I honestly didn't even know what we were arguing about. I felt useless. I felt like I wasn't a proper man because I couldn't keep her happy or satisfied. Don't get me wrong there would be times, especially in the beginning, when she was amazing,

loving, caring, kind, almost manic really when I look back, telling me I was the best partner in the world and saying that nobody had ever made her feel like how I did. Over time this just got less and less though and her complaints got more and more. I was starting to crumble. My work was suffering, I was stressed, frazzled, anxious and depressed.

My parents had split up when I was eight and I grew up watching my own mother struggle. Dad had been a gambler and had walked out on us. It was always important to me that I stick things out and look after my partner. My mother never had that and I remember how difficult that was for her. She was depressed and suicidal whilst we were growing up. My dad had just walked away and given up on us all. I vowed never to do that. It was very painful for me to see Jane unhappy or angry. I wanted to make it all OK but she reinforced the idea that her unhappiness and dissatisfaction was my fault and my responsibility. If I ever said anything, she would tell me I had issues and that I needed to see a therapist. Sounds a bit mad now, in retrospect I know. In the end, I made an appointment to see a psychologist in desperation and in total despair, not knowing how I could be getting things so wrong. I didn't know what was going on anymore. I was so glad I went at that time.

Luckily I saw a therapist who understood narcissism. I explained my current situation and how truly terrible I was feeling. I felt stuck and hopeless. I felt totally to blame. The therapist quickly identified that the issues were not just mine, but of the relationship. I learnt a lot in therapy about what a healthy relationship is. It takes two. I brought a lot of stuff into the relationship, especially with my strong and rather rigid views of what it means to be a man. I know now that am not completely responsible for her or anyone elses happiness. I am also not completely responsible for their mood, or their behaviours. Even though I kind of knew that back then, I felt responsible. My self-esteem was at an all time low when I was basically ordered to go to therapy by Jane – in a way to appease her needs. It ultimately was the best thing I did. It was painful at times, but with the help of the therapist I came to understand how some of my own earlier experiences, with what I saw my mother go through, had really distorted my sense of what a healthy relationship is. I also had assumed responsibilities that were not mine. I was trying to control. I have now learnt to take care of my own needs and to take care of myself first and foremost. I've learnt that relationships take two people and that it is not only unfair for anybody to blame you constantly, in the way that Jane had done, but that it is abusive. I had never thought I would find myself in an abusive relationship, but I did. In time, it wore my confidence and self-esteem down. By working on my self-esteem and learning healthy boundaries I was able to end the destructive relationship with Jane. We had been together for five years and were engaged to be married. I had bought her a big expensive engagement ring that she then sold. Within months after we split, she was already with somebody else. This only reinforced my belief and relief that I had done the right thing. I am now with a wonderful woman who is loving and supportive and loves me for me and I enjoy a healthy and respectful relationship."

By arming yourself with information about narcissism and narcissistic abuse you can take a huge and pivotal perspective shift. Hopefully this is one that shifts from believing, *'it's me'* and *'my fault'*… to understanding that actually this is more so what it *feels* like to be in a relationship with a narcissist. These beliefs and feelings are symptoms of being in an unhealthy, toxic relationship. In many cases, those who have experienced narcissistic abuse arrive at therapy feeling like they are losing themselves and their mind. If you relate to this, I'd like to assure you that whilst it may feel like that sometimes, it's likely not the case. This kind of relationship dynamic is in itself the very thing that can leave you feeling like you are going crazy. It is a symptom of dysfunction. Chances are once you are able to bring an end to any toxic or abusive relationships, your sense of sanity will quite rapidly be restored.

Reading, studying, learning all you can about this kind of abuse and associated issues is an essential early step in recovery. If anything, it helps you start to come to some understanding as to why somebody may be like this in the first place. How that is not your fault, that it's not your responsibility and how you can work on yourself, *for yourself*, in order to heal and move on. You can enjoy healthier, more rewarding and fulfilling relationships. Educating and informing yourself about this subject area also importantly helps with the cognitive processing of your experience. It can help provide some explanation, perhaps answer some questions – although perhaps not all. It may support you in starting to make some sense of what can often otherwise feel like a very maddening, non-sensical situation. It can help your process of letting go of any need to control, to make the narcissist see or understand, or to try and change them. For many people, coming to realise for the first time you are, or have been involved with a narcissist is quite a shock. Arming yourself with information about this whole subject area is important and helpful, however, it is equally crucial you go gently with yourself...

Reflection points:

* How did you first come to suspect or realise you may have been involved/ or are involved with a narcissist?
* What are some of the behaviours or actions you recognised that led you to consider this?
* What negative effects has this relationship had on you?
* What do you understand about narcissists and narcissism at this point?
* What might be helpful for you at this stage?
* Any further thoughts or reflections?

8.

Spotting the signs – become an expert narcissist spotter

AWARENESS IS KEY TO CHANGE

One of the steps in recovering from narcissistic abuse and breaking any pattern of being drawn to, or equally attracting people with narcissistic traits, is to become an expert 'Narcissist Spotter'. Ideally, you will be able to recognise and spot the signs and traits of a narcissist from at least a hundred yards away. In our modern society, narcissistic traits can be seen everywhere. Our modern individualistic culture arguably breeds a certain kind of selfishness and self-seeking interests. You probably wouldn't need to spend too long on social media platforms to be able to spot them. Social media is a perfect playground for the most self-absorbed, self-obsessed, attention-seekers amongst us in desperate need of admiration. It's an ideal place for narcissists to seek and secure a reliable *narcissistic supply* (ie. attention, admiration, praise from others). Social media is also a place where this is absolutely normalised.

We also live in an increasingly less positive interdependent society where instead, individualism, competition, goal-focused achievement, financial and consumerist 'success' are highly regarded, usually over more nourishing values. This is clearly apparent in the rise of the celebrity culture over the last decade or so where the fame-hungry aspire for acknowledgement, attention, money and fame, often with such a strong drive to 'make it' that there is little regard for the impact their ambitions might have on other people, on their values or integrity. Many young people now claim to aspire to being 'famous' for nothing much in particular. Cultural changes of this kind over recent times serve as a breeding ground for narcissism. That's certainly not to say that anybody with drive or ambition or all celebrities are narcissists. Nor are narcissistic traits the same as being out and out personality disordered. Arguably we all have some element of these traits to some extent, however, a true narcissist will typically have very little, if any, capacity to self-reflect and recognise or be concerned about their narcissistic ways. Narcissists do not care about any impact their selfish actions have on others. If they do, it's usually disingenuous or with the sole purpose of manipulation.

So basically, narcissists can be found anywhere and everywhere. Male or female, young or old, they can be hard to spot to the untrained eye, and that is why so many people find themselves in relationships, at work, in friendships, or otherwise involved with them – and then suffer the price for it. Anybody who has experienced a relationship of any kind with a narcissist will know first hand how completely abusive, unhealthy and traumatising it can be. If you have had such experience, it is really important to learn how to spot a narcissist and where possible, stay away from them, or if that is impossible (eg. at work or family) find ways to manage situations and yourself so that you have as little involvement with them as possible. Firm boundaries are crucial and that along with how to manage your feelings and communication are covered in later chapters.

THE SIGNS:

Traditionally, overt narcissists are often very charismatic, charming, manipulative and seductive in their ways. More sinister or covert traits can be harder to spot, particularly as it is so easy to be blindsided by all the initial overload of love-bombing, the alluring qualities, compliments, gifts, enticements and actions. These behaviours in themselves however are often the first warning signs to look out for. When you first meet a narcissist they will be looking to see if you are somebody that can adequately feed their narcissistic supply. That is, can you offer the level and consistency of admiration and attention they so desperately need in order to support their fragile ego state and for them to maintain enough sense of self-worth and self-esteem to survive. It is so vital for a narcissist to receive a constant supply of attention and adoration that they will go to any lengths to charm, manipulate or bully in order to get this. They will spread their ongoing search wide and far.

Their attempts to achieve this often involve 'love-bombing' in the early days. Love-bombing tactics include compliments, being showered with gifts, appearing to be deeply attentive and thoughtful (for example taking note of some interests you like such as a band or theatre show and then presenting you with tickets). For the more overt type of narcissist, they may rely on bragging and exaggerating about their successes, finances or status in order to impress. In romantic situations this can include declarations of love very early on, discussions or declarations of long-term plans such as weddings, moving in together or having children. Discussing long-term relationship plans or declaring that this is 'the one' or that this will be a long term affair within days of meeting is often a warning sign for commitment issues – which most narcissists have. The covert narcissist or one that can be a little trickier to spot will play on their 'vulnerabilities' or play 'victim' in order to seduce or pull you into rescuing, caring or taking some responsibility for them. This is simply another form of them attempting to obtain narcissistic supply. Any kind of attention is simply attention for a narcissist. Here they may play up how misunderstood or how badly treated they have been. These types tend to have an unfortunate string of 'psycho' or 'abusive' exes. The narcissist can be spotted by determining how much, if any, responsibility they may take in their part in it all. I tend to think it is quite suspicious if somebody has a long string of psycho or bad-exes. There is usually a common denominator.

Any self-respecting narcissist will be aiming to make you feel special and unique in whichever way they can. This is recognised by comments such as: *"we have such a powerful connection"*, *"we are meant to be"*, *"nobody has ever loved me like you do"* *(and vice versa) "nobody has ever made me laugh like you do"*, *"I've never felt this way before... this is so different"*, *"you are such an amazing and smart colleague, I can really learn a lot from you"*, *"nobody has ever understood or known me like you do"*, *"I've never been this turned on"* and *"I've never felt anything like this before... this must really be what true love is"*.

All of these comments and actions are understandably quite lovely and flattering to hear yet essentially designed to assess for the level of narcissistic supply you may be able to offer. Are you somebody who can be easily pulled into a level of fantasy about the relationship? Or can you stay grounded and keep it real? That, for me, makes a huge difference to how easily it is to get lost under the narcissistic spell. Their assessment is achieved via an overwhelm of romance and impressive claims or by portraying themselves as the misunderstood victim and pulling on heart strings. Bear in mind a narcissist will only be seeking for what you or anybody else can offer them. They generally will only be considering connecting with people who can offer then some gains and who they can get something from. Whether that be a consistent and ample narcissistic supply, financial gains, emotional support, somebody to blame and shame, social connections, status, work, and the such. Sorry to break any romantic fantasy here but if it feels too good to be true, it more than likely is. If it's too much too soon, that is also a fair warning sign. Take heed. Keep grounded and keep it real.

Healthy relationships take time to be nurtured. It takes time to build trust and to truly get to know somebody. Too much too soon is a sign there may be a narcissist around.

It is understandably very easy to get swept away in the powerful romance and wooing of the early stages. Learning the signs and mastering how to spot them is a key step and fortunately one of those things that once you can see them, it will be very hard to be 'unsee' and be caught again. As long as you continue to master how to pay attention and remain vigilant to the warning signs!

So how do I learn to spot these traits and become a narcissist-spotting expert?

It takes being able to conduct a **grounded, honest** and **objective** appraisal of what people in your life say and what people in your life do. Actions speak louder than words. If another persons words and actions do not match, that is a warning sign. Be sure to look at the actions and do not just believe words. An apology is an action, not just a word. The chapters of this book so far has covered what narcissism is and includes defining characteristics. Below is a further list of traits and behaviours synonymous with narcissism in order to help you learn to spot them.

* Extreme self-interest. Narcissists will easily talk about themselves and their interests all day long. They will rarely ask you any meaningful questions about you or your life. A good indicator you have met a narcissist is if you notice they often don't even ask how you are. They will though however,

happily and easily talk about themselves and their interests all day long.

* Thanks to social media, it's now easier to spot attention seeking narcissists as indicated by endless selfies and attention-seeking posts. Especially easy to spot when they are consistently the only person in the shot. Overtly sexually provocative, purposely intriguing shots or posts, or posts highlighting wealth or power are also usually a reliable indicator of narcissism.

* Name dropping and 'topping'. If you've met or know somebody famous, or been to a great restaurant, you can guarantee your narcissist friend or partner has met somebody even more famous and frequents even better eateries than you could ever find.

* They will boast of their own talents and achievements and belittle, criticise and judge others. They will point out others flaws or weaknesses in a bid to exaggerate their own accomplishments and to feel better about themselves.

* When you first meet a narcissist they are often highly complimentary, charming and friendly. They may even buy you gifts and take you to exciting and interesting places. The aim is to make you feel 'special', however, their real motivation is to manipulate a response that ultimately caters to their needs.

* They will make all sorts of romantic and wonderful promises to hook you in with hope, yet their actions will not match their words.

* If and when anybody does not offer them or maintain the level of constant adoration, admiration or attention they require, they quickly turn hostile, punishing or being abusive, cutting the victim off from the social group, finding ways to sack or dump them, spread rumours about them, be cutting to them, give them the silent treatment, etc.

* Remember: Actions speak louder than words.

"When I first met Mike, he was incredibly attentive and romantic. He showered me with compliments and gifts, even whisking me away for a romantic break to Paris shortly after we met. He ticked all the boxes, I really believed I had found the 'one' – my Prince Charming. He had an air of elusiveness about him, which I found quite intriguing. It pulled me in. I wanted to be the one to really know and understand him – to love him. And for him to love me. In hindsight, it was only a matter of months, possibly weeks if I'm really honest, before he started acting selfishly and the digs and negative comments started. He was selfish and looking back, I would say, quite insecure. He would make digs about my body, or income and at the same time brag about his fitness or how much he earned. It was hard to recognise at the time as the negatives were barely detectable amongst the good times. Sometimes he'd say something mean and it was so out there, that I wasn't even sure if I'd heard it correctly. I couldn't understand. I also felt like I was stuck at believing the man I first met. My first impressions of him were so powerful they kind of just stuck. I felt increasingly confused the meaner he was to me, as when we first met he was so perfect. I just couldn't make sense how this could be the same person... I lost trust in my own judgement... and it took me time before I was able to find perspective again."

Reflection point:

Looking back, what were the signs you noticed or perhaps overlooked when you first met any narcissistic partner in your life?

* How did you feel at the time?
* How did their actions not match their words or promises?
* What (if anything) stopped you from taking heed of any warning signs? (This can be helpful to identify for later stages of recovery and for the future).
* How might you recognise a narcissist in future? What would be the signs you would look out for and spot?
* What would help you to recognise this in the future? Try to think of as many helpful factors as you can.

ACTIONS SPEAK LOUDER THAN WORDS

The phrase "actions speak louder than words" could not be any more true for helping yourself recognise the related behaviour and endless broken promises of a narcissist. Many of us get fooled, or pulled back by the allure, temptations, apologies and promises of a narcissist. Interestingly, such is the dynamic that they tend to be more forthcoming, elaborate, manipulative and convincing the more they sense you pulling away from them.

> *"Ian and I had talked about starting a family. I have always wanted children but I'd spent many years focusing on my career. When it came to my mid-30's I realised just how much I wanted a baby. I had been seeing Ian on and off for about 5 or 6 years by this point. Right from early on he would talk about us being parents, we would joke about who they might take after and how we would be wonderful parents. In hindsight I can see*

more clearly now that he didn't mean it and was always a little uncomfortable when plans got serious. Clearly committing to a family would never suit his spontaneous lifestyle and need for freedom. There was many, many times during our relationship when he would suddenly leave, declaring that he needed 'space'. We were constantly on and off – almost on a weekly basis. He would disappear for days or weeks and then reappear. That just became the way the relationship was. What I find so cruel though is that he would be so erratic around my desires to have children – he knew how much this meant to me. I guess he used to say all the right things, what I wanted to hear, but his actions didn't match up.

There were times that he would refuse to have sex, saying that I was being disgusting and desperate for being the one to initiate and ask for it. Other times he would complain I never made the first move?! I felt confused and horrible. With no success of pregnancy after trying for a year or so I made appointments for IVF consultations. He would swing from being really keen to then disappearing and leaving for days, missing appointments, leaving me on my own to see the doctors. It was so embarrassing and confusing to understand at the time, but I guess I was so set on being pregnant I made excuses for his erratic behaviour. He would miss appointments, make excuses for not being there, or just go awol at the last minute. I know it sounds mad, but he always seemed to be the victim each time and I would end up empathising with him and his struggles. Or being left feeling guilty. On one occasion he explained he had not been able to meet at our IVF appointment as he'd been helping an elderly lady who had her bag stolen on the way. I'm not even sure if that happened but if I gave any hint of disbelief he would react violently and leave me feeling like I was a terrible person for doubting him. Or worse still, he would create huge conflict and argue – and as usual, I'd end up feeling guilty and that it was my fault. I'd done or not done something to make him angry. I was a bag of nerves at the time. I actually think I was too much of a nervous wreck and in ill physical health because of my nerves to have gotten pregnant at the time anyway! It sounds ridiculous now, but this went on for years and although we got along to speak to the staff at the clinic we never actually got started with treatment.

At times I really felt like I'd had enough and I'd make attempts to end the relationship. Again, with hindsight, I can see now that these were the times that he would ramp up the discussions about us being parents and starting a family together and I would be pulled back in. I would be pulled back into the hope of it all again, the dream that things would be different this time... that we would get pregnant and be a family. Starting to see things more objectively helped me to start to see that's all it ever was... a fantasy. He used my desire to be a mother to pull me back in again and again and not let me go and then he would break up and disappear again, on a regular basis. This went on for years. It was unbelievably cruel.

With help, I eventually found the strength to leave Ian. But now I'm in my 40s I am coming to terms with the fact that I will probably never have my own children now. I bitterly regret the years I wasted believing he meant what he said. In some ways, a part of me still does believe, or wants to believe that he did want children with me. Maybe a part of him did and he was too scared – too scared of the commitment – I don't know. I see now though that if he truly wanted to, he would have and it would have happened. Ironically, as much as I'd love to be a mum I'm actually grateful that I did not have children with him. He would have been too inconsistent for the sort of parenting I would like. I wouldn't want that ongoing for more years for me or my child.

I regret allowing myself to get sidetracked by all the lies and the stories. I see now, at the end of the day, that if he really

*wanted something he would put the work in to make it happen
and even though he said all the right things at the right times,
the actions and the efforts were not there. I just wish I'd seen
it sooner. During this time, I have seen many of my friends
become mothers. I needed to take responsibility for myself and
my wasted years in that relationship."*

When we suspect we are in any kind of a relationship with a narcissist it is crucial that we evaluate their actions and behaviours, rather than just their words. Any abusive narcissist will be highly skilled at manipulating others to get their own needs met. This means saying all the right things, at the right times. This is something they sadly would have probably learnt from very early on in their lives. It will be second nature to them to instinctively tune into whatever buttons they feel need to be pressed in order to get their needs met. They will attune to all kinds of vulnerabilities in others so they are able to say just the thing in order to pull on someones heart strings, trigger feelings of guilt or shame, fear or anxiety, all in order to manipulate and control. I often hear people complain that the narcissist did this, or the narcissist did that, that it was the narcissist who wasted their time, wasted years, made them move or made them do things they didn't want to. Continuing to blame the narcissist for everything is maintaining a victim mentality. That is not helpful if you want to move on. In recovery, it is really important to learn to take full responsibility for yourself and your actions. Please note, taking responsibility for yourself is not the same as beating yourself up! Don't be hard on yourself – you have been through enough! Don't continue the punishment! Taking responsibility for yourself means considering your part in things. Look at what you choose and what you do. Nobody has total power to make you do things or make you feel a certain way. You have a part in it. You have a choice. It is your choice as to whether you believe the narcissists lies or manipulation or if you look at their actions and make your own decision from there. We have to watch what they are doing and saying and identify any discrepancies, whilst also staying close to our own internal experience. Watching for your own thoughts, feelings, reactions, sensations or triggers. It may be helpful to work with a therapist to help identify what they are for yourself and perhaps recognise where that has come from originally. Awareness is key.

Reflection point:

* What were the times when the narcissist in your life has promised or said things only for their actions to go against that or go in opposition to that?
* How often did/does this happen?
* How did/does this leave you feeling?
* In the past, what would you have done at these times?
* How might you do things differently? What is more helpful to you now?
* How can you take responsibility for yourself?
* What is the most loving thing you can do for yourself now?

9. A Perfect Match

Relationships outside of ourselves obviously involve at least one other person. Therefore, it would be unfair, unhelpful and unhealthy for the focus to remain solely on the narcissist. Just like with story of Narcissus and Echo, the narcissist is not the only part of the relationship equation.

There does seem to be a certain partner 'profile' that is both attracted to, and attractive for the narcissist. There is a seemingly deep invisible, magnetic pull between narcissist and somebody that is in many ways, a perfect match to facilitate a narcissistic partners selfish, self-seeking, 'all-about-me' ways. Generally, speaking, this tends to be the kind of person who will tend to put other peoples needs before their own, or in a variety of ways, not attend appropriately to their own wants or needs. Perhaps they feel that by doing so they are somehow being selfish, even experiencing guilt for taking care of themselves or putting themselves first. There can be a sense of martyrdom in being largely or completely without needs and selfless. Many of us dangerously mistake this for being 'strong' or perhaps even 'easygoing'. This idea is often something we learn from our own families whilst we were growing up, during childhood and adolescence. These dysfunctional ways of being in relationships are often modelled by our parents or other significant figures in our lives. Perhaps there was or still is a family message that is inherited about self-care, what it means to be 'selfish' and about how we should be in relationships. We learn a lot about relationships from our parents, family and early life experiences. Whilst our early experiences can really shape our tendency in relationships this by no way means that it cannot be changed. We can certainly learn and work towards enjoying healthier and more fulfilling relationships as adults regardless of any earlier messages we may have adopted from our family.

People in potentially abusive relationships often state they feel like they 'lose themselves' as their focus becomes more and more about the 'other'. Much like the echoist, they begin to shrink into the shadows and lose their voice. The loss of self and focus on the other reflects issues of personal boundaries, self-esteem and self-worth. Ultimately it's reflective of the relationship you have within yourself. From my experience, partners of narcissists tend to be some of the kindest, most caring, supportive, forgiving, trusting and understanding people you could ever wish to meet. They are also often intelligent, high-achieving and successful. This in part, adds to the frustration and confusion I have often witnessed in clients during the early stages of therapy, where it's hard for one to make sense of how they have ended up in such a destructive relationship. However, being very driven, ambitious and achievement-focused in itself often comes at a price of neglecting your own self-compassion and self-care needs to some extent. Many of the clients I have worked who have experienced narcissistic abuse are some of the most effective people I have ever met. They make fantastic project managers, trouble-shooters or event organisers. They know how to get things done. They are often very practical, logical, goal-focused achievers, sometimes, perhaps verging on work addiction or 'busy-holism' – they are 'do-ers'. Keeping so busy, however, can be to the detriment of really identifying, tuning into and attending to your own deep self-care needs and wants. It is also not uncommon for partners of narcissists to be quite self-punishing and hard on themselves. This is explored in more detail in a later chapter on 'self-talk'.

Many of the personality traits and characteristics of those of us who are drawn to narcissists are synonymous with that of *codependency* or sometimes also referred to as *echoism* – from the Greek mythology. Codependency is essentially about unhealthy, dysfunctional relationship issues. A lot of literature on the subject of codependency centres around the idea of the partner being alcoholic or addict, in opposed to 'the narcissist' but I think it is much of a muchness. Codependency also encompasses relationship addiction – characterised by aspects of preoccupation or dependence on the other person, be it psychologically, emotionally, socially, financially and/or physically. Another key feature of codependency is an over focus on taking care of others and in the process of doing so, forgetting or disregarding the importance of taking care of yourself. This can cause a range of distressing interpersonal and identity issues.

Many people regard codependency as simply meaning being completely dependent on the alcoholic or addicted partner as well as generally a 'need to be needed' by them. That is a rather simplistic understanding. I believe codependency is more than that and the specific presentations of codependent traits are unique to each individual. The term codependency typically captures the *caretaker, people pleaser* and *fixer* partner in the relationship dynamic. There is a distinct lack of boundaries with codependency and a common belief is that others have to be OK in order for partners to feel OK in themselves – "if they're ok then I'm ok". The inability to manage your own anxieties or emotions is often what fuels an over focus on trying to make sure everybody else, or the narcissist, is fine. Hence the attempts of rescuing and control. Echoism is a term more specific to narcissistic abuse although the parallels are similar. Whilst not personally so concerned about labels it may be that reading and learning about codependency recovery may also aid recovery and healing from narcissistic abuse. There is certainly a lot in the literature and in the 12 step programme of codependence anonymous. This can help support the development of self-awareness, the processing of experience, the learning and development of healthy boundaries and other interpersonal aspects that can support healthy relationships. (please search for codependence anonymous (CODA) for more information or to find your nearest support meetings). The support from a group setting can also be an added help at this time.

In general terms, I think it is helpful to understand codependency as basically being about unhealthy and dysfunctional relationships. Healthy relationships start with yourself first and foremost. If you have this right, then all other relationships become a lot easier. Codependents have a tendency to be more concerned with how others are doing, than they are about themselves. They tend to find it easier to recognise and attend to the needs and wants of those around them, whilst neglecting their own needs or wants and struggle to take good care of themselves. They find it easier to identify how others feel but struggle to identify or sit with emotions in themselves. They will often sacrifice their own needs or wants in favour of supporting their partners and have an over-sense of responsibility. Issues of codependency can really interfere with your ability to enjoy healthy and fulfilling relationships. Obviously echosim and codependency type traits are a perfect match for narcissists as narcissists will inherently want it to be all about them. They will seek out partners who are happy for it to be all about them and who will volunteer to care, justify and take responsibility for the narcissists wants, needs and behaviours in various ways.

Remember for the narcissist, it's *all about them* and they need the focus to be that way in their preferred relationships. Unsurprisingly then, they intrinsically seek out and look to attract partners with whom this focus and dynamic suits and works for. In other words, narcissists seek out and find partners in those who are quite comfortable and happy for the attention and focus to be on the other. The type of partner who is attractive to, and will most likely find themselves in relationship with a narcissist, consistently forsake their own needs or wants in order to support or appease their partners. Sometimes this is because putting others first and above is viewed as admirable. Some people feel that putting themselves first is selfish or out of order. You may mistake neglecting or sacrificing your own needs or having poor boundaries as being 'easygoing'. Sometimes the kind of over-care or over-responsibility in unhealthy relationships is misunderstood as simply being caring or altruistic, perhaps even with a martyr-like quality to it. As previously mentioned, this could be something that has been learnt early on in childhood, modelled or inherited from our own families as an ideal way to be. I personally regard this as being highly dangerous and unhealthy. It associates with a loss of sense of self, lack of personal identify, issues around boundaries, codependency, echoism, trauma and ultimately acts as a powerful magnetic pull to a narcissist.

If you wish to recover from narcissistic abuse and importantly avoid repeating this kind of relationship pattern, its imperative you start to *bring your focus back to yourself.* Recovery involves looking to develop a loving, supportive, compassionate and kind relationship with *yourself* first and foremost.

When you have a good, healthy inner relationship with yourself, all other relationships become much easier

Characteristics and traits commonly recognised in those in abusive, narcissistic and unhealthy relationships:

✳ Overly caring and concerned for the welfare of others. Often this is easier than caring for yourself. Clearly care and concern for others is a lovely quality to have, however this is a concern if this is to the detriment or neglect of your own care.

* Is a 'do-er'. Is *the* go-to person to get things done.
* A caretaker or rescuer.
* Highly emotionally sensitive. Easily being able to sense into, empathise, recognise or even predict others moods or emotional pain – although has difficulty identifying this for themselves.
* A tendency or preference to be quite logical and practical, preferring to use or find it easier to rely on logic and the rational mind than emotional, felt-sense or gut instinct.
* Can feel quite 'disconnected' or numb or zone-out at times.
* Have difficulty identifying their own feelings or needs.
* Feel responsible, or believe in some way that they are responsible for helping, changing or fixing others.
* High-aiming, achievement oriented or focused.
* Feels guilty, bad, anxious or responsible if others are upset.
* Are kind and forgiving to others, but not so much to themselves.
* Self-esteem issues. Feel a sense of not 'doing enough', 'being enough' or being 'not good enough'.
* Does not recognise or accept the unavailability of those they are attracted to.
* Deny or minimise their own feelings.
* Are hard on themselves. Have a punitive, negative inner 'self-talk'.
* Confuse having no or little personal needs as 'being strong' or 'easygoing'.
* Are very hard-working and driven.
* People pleasers. Negating own needs for the sake of others.
* Rely on others or external factors (eg. work, studies, partners, children) too much for their sense of identify or self-esteem.
* Being or feeling isolated.
* A desire to 'fix' or heal the wounds in others.

* Have a high tolerance for stress and abuse.
* Have difficulty identifying your own wants/likes/needs/thoughts/feelings.
* Believe that putting yourselves first somehow means being selfish or disloyal.
* Experience discomfort or guilt when taking care of or treating yourself.
* Endure or persevere with difficult or abusive situations/relationships (survival mentality).
* Over-busy careers/work/personal lives.
* Have difficulty saying 'No'.
* Endure and stay in harmful relationships confusing tolerance for abuse as being loyal, dedicated, caring or selfless.
* Have trouble identifying, setting or holding personal boundaries.
* Having read the previous line think to themselves 'I'm not really sure what my boundaries are'.
* Regard being so concerned/preoccupied/focused on the caring of others as being altruistic and selfless.
* Will cater to other peoples needs but neglect their own or deny they even have any.
* Find it difficult to ask others for help or to show vulnerability.
* Make excuses or justify the abusive and inappropriate behaviours of others.
* Take responsibility or feel responsible for the actions or feelings of others
* Low self-esteem.
* Denial patterns – deny their own feelings, deny their partners abusive comments or actions.
* Find it difficult to accept compliments, recognition or gifts.
* Compromise own values, wants, needs and integrity for the sake of partner/others.
* Have an over-sense of responsibility.

* Believe you can somehow control or change other people – partners, family members, colleagues or friends.
* Experience a disconnect or ignore or mistrust any internal felt-sense and gut instinct about what feels right or wrong.
* Have/had a parent or other family member that was a narcissist or addict.
* Fear of partners mood, anger, rage, reaction (this is often rooted from earlier life experiences).
* Have difficulty communicating you own needs or wants, likes or dislikes.
* Feeling like you have 'lost your voice'.
* Experience confusion.
* Doubt yourself – especially in response to partners comments or gas-lighting.
* Have feelings of guilt and shame.
* Are used to having to be 'strong' and/or are 'the strong one'.
* Feel like 'it's me', 'it's my fault', 'I'm responsible'.
* Feel like 'I'm going mad'.

Reflection point:

* What characteristics or traits do you relate to or recognise in yourself?
* How might this play a role in your relationships?

CONSIDERING YOUR OWN NARCISSISM

An important point for consideration and one that I think often gets missed is considering your own narcissism. That might read a little strange but it is important. Lets be real here... everybody can be a little selfish or narcissistic sometimes. Also, as previously explained, there is a scale. At one end of the spectrum is a more usual experience where some people may have some narcissistic traits some times. At the extreme end of the scale is pathological narcissistic personality disorder. Narcissistic *defences* describe narcissistic-like behaviours, actions or interpersonal exchanges that many of us can demonstrate without it meaning we are complete and utter narcissists. Usually these defences are triggered in response to feeling threatened, frightened or insecure in some way. By narcissistic defences I mean times, when feeling insecure or less than, one may then become very judgemental and critical about others. Or be arrogant, belittling or haughty. The behaviours may not be our usual way of being, however they can appear when we are feeling particularly defensive. We may not be aware we are doing this all of the times this happens either because like many narcissistic ways, they are defences that serve to protect a fragile sense of self. In the case of narcissistic defences these tend to effectively kick-in at times of vulnerability.

During the reading of this book so far, have you have wondered or worried that you might be a narcissist at all? If so, have you genuinely felt concerned about the impact of that on other people? If you have, then chances are you are probably not a narcissist at all! Real narcissists are not able to self-reflect very honestly. They wouldn't be too concerned about the impact their actions have on others either. They would not easily be able to consider (or care) how they might affect other people. Wondering about your own narcissism is a normal and healthy part of the process. I believe it is also a very helpful part of the process to spend some time considering this. For many of us, there is room for further objective and honest self-reflection – this supports our personal growth. Most of us are capable of some narcissism in small doses. That's not of huge concern. However, I do want to shine a light on any traits of narcissism that may interfere with your recovery process.

Empathy is something a narcissist lacks. Partners of narcissists however tend to overcompensate for this in the relationship. They are usually overly empathic, often mistaking this for just being caring, sensitive or attuned. This is one area that has the potential to get in the way of your recovery if it is too extreme. I think it is a little narcissistic to believe you somehow have special powers, insight or ability to understand, help, control or change the narcissist – or anybody else for that matter. Healthy empathy means being able to recognise and acknowledge how others are feeling and to communicate that, showing them you care. But it is not taking on any of those feelings for them, or trying to change or fix that for them – that is called codependency. Codependency is not healthy.

Arrogance and entitlement are also narcissistic traits that have the potential to interfere with your recovery process. Believing that you already know it all in any way is probably not going to help you to move on or to heal the trauma and recover from narcissistic abuse. Recovery takes humility. Recovery takes honesty and being in touch with your vulnerability. It can take time to feel safe enough to do that. Learning to slow down and be gentle and compassionate with yourself helps.

Narcissists do not take responsibility for themselves. Instead they seek out partners who will take responsibility for them on their behalf. Believing you are responsible for another persons behaviours, choices or feelings is unhealthy. Again, I would argue that can also seem a bit narcissistic. Does anybody have that amount of power? What other people do or do not do is not within your control. You do not have that power. Believing you do is not helpful. In recovery it is important to focus on what *is* your responsibility and what is within your control. And more importantly to know what *is not* so that this aspect is not simply another variation of narcissism. Narcissists will want to portray themselves as a victim and continue to not take responsibility for themselves. Please be mindful you do not assume this position.

Nobody can force you to have feelings or to behave in any way. You are responsible for you.

Some questions to help honestly consider your own narcissism include:

* Do I believe I am special and different?
* Do I feel misunderstood because most people are not skilled or intelligent enough to understand me?
* Do I dominate conversations?
* Do I feel more interesting, intelligent, more experienced or insightful than everybody else?
* Am I judgemental about other people, places or things?
* Do I believe I have the power to control or change the narcissist in my life? Or to change anybody else?
* Can I come across as arrogant, dismissive or rude at times?
* Do I use money, beauty, affection, intelligence or status to feel power over or control others?
* Do I have a sense of entitlement and expect to be treated differently?
* Do I seek gains or special treatment by portraying myself as a victim?
* Can I be arrogant and think that I know best or more than others?
* Do I exaggerate my achievements, status, progress or connections?
* Do I make things up?
* Do I lie to get what I want?
* Can I get jealous, resentful or competitive with others?

As I say, we all have an element of narcissism. Narcissistic defences can show at times too – usually when we feel insecure or threatened. This is not anything to freak out about, however spending time to honestly and objectively reflect about your beliefs, behaviours and motivations can help develop the very traits narcissists have difficulty with. So finding a balance with the following areas can also help support your own recovery; empathy, appropriate levels of responsibility, appropriate consideration, honesty, humility, compassion and authenticity.

10.

Considering the origins of attraction

CHILDREN OF NARCISSISTS

Many parents, especially narcissistic parents, will install in their children a firm and clear message that positive regard, feedback, acceptance or love is based on conditions. From this kind of parenting, children learn they are acceptable or worthy on the basis of what they do or achieve rather than feeling accepted for who they are. Unsurprisingly then children of narcissistic parents often experience a sense of low self-worth. Through conditional love and regard children absorb a message that they are *'not good enough'* just the way they are and that they need to do more or be better in order to receive the acceptance or love they desire and deserve. They can feel, *'not worthy'* or *'unlovable'* on some level. Positive regard from a narcissist is conditional. Attention and affection is therefore offered depending on what you do, rather than who you are. Regard becomes dependent on your achievements rather than your personal qualities. Children of narcissists then tend to respond to that early message of futile and impossible expectation. Core beliefs of *'I'm not good enough'*, *'I'm unworthy'* or *'It's my fault'* are touched on and triggered again in adult narcissistic relationships. Those who find themselves repeating destructive adult relationship patterns with narcissistic partners may find that at the core is a subconscious repeating of earlier relational dynamics. In other words, a replication of the role they assumed with a parent or other family member where perhaps the other person was dominant or abusive and as a child we submitted, complied, appeased or assumed responsibility in order to survive or manage the situation.

In my clinical work, generally speaking I have seen that children of narcissists will either strive on bravely and often rather manically, in a futile fight to do, to be or to feel *'enough'* or *'good enough'*. They've become highly driven, over-achievers. Paradoxically others respond in quite the opposite way. Some people submit and give up any ambition or expectation to be *'good enough'* or to ever *'achieve or do enough'* in the eyes of their parent/s. Those who rebel and opt for the latter tend to struggle with self-esteem issues in a slightly different way. They tend to wrestle with shame-based problems and are likely to develop issues such as addictions or eating disorders. Children of narcissists can understandably demonstrate narcissistic tendencies too. As to be expected, given this has been modelled by one or both parents. Aspects of narcissistic *defence* are commonly seen in those with addictions and restrictive eating disorders such as anorexia nervosa.

As a slight aside, I believe there are people wrongly diagnosed as having personality disorders, addictions, eating disorders, clinical depression, obsessive compulsive disorder (OCD) or other clinical psychiatric diagnosis when in fact, they are simply wrestling with the struggles of having or still being in a relationship with a narcissist, specifically having a narcissistic parent. These conditions can be the symptom, not the cause. I do not believe anybody develops any of these issues randomly, for no reason. It is often symptomatic of all that comes from having a narcissistic parent. These behaviours then serve as maladaptive coping strategies. The issues lie deeper and elsewhere. Unfortunately, the wrong diagnosis tragically continues the harmful and inaccurate underlying belief that has already been absorbed. That being; *'It's me', 'It's my fault', 'There's something wrong with me", "I'm not good enough"* and so on.

Having a narcissistic parent feels a lot like having a narcissistic partner. It leaves us doubting ourselves, feeling guilt as if we are to blame, as if it's our fault and responsibility. We feel we are unworthy of unconditional love and compassion. This understandably has a huge impact on self-esteem and self-worth. If we have experienced this kind of abuse or neglect growing up it can be quite difficult to detect because it is usually so inherent in the family system. What we grow up with is, for a long time, our world, it is what we consider 'normal'. It is often only as adolescents or adults, that we then start to see the bigger picture and gain a broader perspective of family life and relationships. Growing up with a narcissistic parent has an impact on the development of a sense of self, the learning and development of boundaries and ideas about relationships and the roles we have within them. As with much of our earlier life experiences, it is incredibly shaping to how we view ourselves, our world and everybody in it.

SURVIVAL INSTINCTS GROWING UP

Often those in narcissistic relationships, whether it's a parent or partner, tend to have a heightened alert system and adopt a way of being that is very much either fight, or flight, or oscillating between the two. Our 'fight or flight' response is an innate survival instinct that we all have. In primitive years this served as an essential aid to our survival and evolution. Nowadays, this fight or flight response can be activated in any manner of situations because our baseline stress levels are so much higher. We are so much more stressed and on alert than we need to be that it doesn't take much for this survival instinct to activate. A stressful commute to work can be enough to trigger our primitive fight or flight response! Historically, this response was supposed to be short-term. A survival instinct to get us through immediate threat or danger helps to keep us safe and alive. More often though, particularly if we have experienced earlier kinds of narcissistic abuse, trauma or codependency issues within the family, we adopt survival strategies as a long-term reaction and it becomes a way of being.

In 'flight' mode, we tend to retreat or seek ways in which to escape, avoid, numb or change our experience and reality. A 'flight' response in relation to being around a narcissist or having a parent who is/was narcissistic describes an urge or impulse to get away from the threat or in many cases, the conflict or abuse. This can include wanting to physically run away, get away and hide, avoidance, submission or compliance. It can also include 'flight' from our inner emotional experience and this is achieved through dissociation, numbing or changing our internal experience via the use of drugs, alcohol, sex, keeping endlessly busy and distracted, workaholism or other obsessive, compulsive or addictive actions.

In 'fight' mode we tend to be more energised and have a desire to fight and stand up for ourselves. We may want to pursue end goals, we tend to feel activated in action mode, are very driven and goal-achievement focused. A 'fight' response is charged with energy and drive to achieve or obtain… to battle and to 'win'. People living in 'fight' mode tend to become extremely focused and highly driven. This in many ways serves a useful function. It can benefit enough to achieve, to obtain good grades, qualifications, careers and financial gains that in turn can offer an element of freedom in some ways from more difficult pasts or situations. The fight reaction and extreme drive force also can keep us away from feeling too much emotional pain and instead leave us feeling empowered and with a sense of being in control.

We can come away from the felt-sense and connection to difficult and painful emotional and physical feelings and instead come up into our heads and begin to rely on our intellect, logic and rational thinking. This is powerful and very helpful if we, at some point in our past, experienced overwhelming emotions. Operating in *go*-mode and relying more on logic and analytical thinking serves to keep us away to some extent from that rather messy and murky emotional world.

Whilst there are some short-term survival gains from both of these ways of being, both a fight or flight response used in the long-term is detrimental to our health, wellbeing, mental health and quality of life. Both survival modes keep us away to some extent, from our inner emotional experience. Whilst that may be useful in moments of intense pain, shock or trauma, these are not useful long-term strategies. Living in survival mode can lead to problems with addictions, stress, burn out, anxiety, depression and importantly is a factor that happens both as a result of and something that can leave us vulnerable to narcissistic abuse.

It is not uncommon for children of narcissists to unconsciously seek out a similar dynamic in romantic relationships or friendships in adulthood. Many, many adults in relationships with narcissists, overt or covert, have had a parent or influential family member who was in some way narcissistic or had at least some narcissistic traits whilst they were growing up, however mild. Perhaps a parent was punitive, authoritarian, harsh, disciplinarian, scathing at times, rarely pleased or satisfied, didn't offer consistent positive, encouraging feedback, was absent, unavailable or pre-occupied for whatever reason. Perhaps they were uninterested or didn't comfort, nurture or care for their child as they should. Or maybe the dynamic between parents was codependent. Perhaps a parent was an addict or alcoholic to some degree. Any form of addiction is arguably selfish and self-seeking in nature. Many narcissists are active addicts.

If you recognise narcissistic traits in your parent/s, whether that be very apparent or perhaps you are unsure, it can be helpful to spend some time reflecting on the following questions:

* Who do I identify as possibly narcissistic in my family?
* What do I know about their background that may help this to make sense?
* What specific narcissistic traits or behaviours do I recognise in them?
* List any examples or memories that stand out for you that relate to this.
* What was it like for you?
* What kind of message did this person communicate – either directly or indirectly via their words and actions? Consider this in terms of the message in how you or others should; Behave? Be treated? Treat others? Interact and relate? Say? Do? Not Do? What kind of messages did they offer about the world? About yourself? About others?
* How did this leave you feeling about yourself? About other people? The opposite sex? About the world?
* Does this relate to any of your relationships as an adult?
* How old were you when you have your earliest memory of a parent being abusive, neglectful or unsupportive?
* What was it like for you at the time? What do you remember?
* What did you as a child need at that time, that you did not receive?
* What did the younger you, the child at that time, need or would have liked to have happen in that moment? What would you have ideally liked somebody to say or do at that time? What reassurance or comfort would the child have liked or needed to have received?
* What would you do now, as an adult, if you witnessed that child experiencing that earlier narcissistic neglect or abuse? If you could go back there now as an adult what you do or say to that child to help them to feel safe, secure, reassured or protected?

* What would you like them to know? (about themselves, the parent, the situation).
* What is it like to perhaps offer that to yourself right now?

Every child deserves to feel safe, secure and to experience unconditional love for who they are, not solely for what they do. Sadly though, this is not always the case. If this is your experience then the one thing I would like you to know is that regardless of the reasons as to why you did not receive the care, protection or nurturing you wanted and indeed deserved as a child... It was not your fault. It cannot be the fault of any child, ever. Because you are a child. If this was the case at all, then the reasons for that would have been because of adult issues. Grown up stuff that belonged to the adults around you. Not the child. Not you. As an adult now, you can begin to offer yourself the care, protection, reassurance, safety, security and unconditional love you deserve, both as a child and an adult. You can learn to reparent, look after and love yourself and your inner child.

11.   Survive, Drive, Thrive

Many of us who experienced narcissism in some form or another, or had a dysfunctional or less than nurturing family life growing up, relate to adopting a survive and/or drive response along the way. Adults living in survival mode are doing whatever it is they feel they need to in order to get by. This involves stifling their own wants and needs, becoming chameleons to give others what we think they want, not holding boundaries, putting up not speaking up and not fulfilling their own potential. Sometimes these survival instincts have been absorbed by what we have learnt early on in life. For example, we learn to stay quiet to avoid conflict at home. We ensure we are 'good' girls or boys and comply or deny. Survival techniques can also utilise the use of mood altering substances or behaviours. In survive and drive, life becomes more about fighting and getting through rather than enjoying or thriving it. Drive reflects extreme determination and high expectations. It is an adapted way of being that focuses on achievement and accomplishments. Drive gives us blinkers. We can become uber-focused on a goal, get busy and get things done yet dangerously ignore or neglect our emotional experience or self-care needs in the midst. It doesn't feel so harmful because along the way we amount achievements and successes that reward our hard work and drive. However, synonymous with drive is an element of being hard on yourself, being punitive and striving for a level of perfection. Like with most things, anything that is too extreme is rarely healthy. Nonetheless, these are ways we adapt and learn to survive and navigate our way through our childhoods. Both variations are actually encouraged to some degree in society and our education systems. Whilst these adopted ways of being have been helpful at an earlier stage they often no longer serve us as adults. More specifically these are ways of being can relate to finding yourself in an adult relationship with a narcissist. Aspects of this can also get in the way of standing up to or leaving a narcissist.

Many people who find themselves experiencing narcissistic abuse are left confused as to how they have found themselves in such a destructive dynamic. Those who are attractive to narcissists tend to be very caring, trusting, nurturing and forgiving. They also usually have a high tolerance to stress. A narcissist will be especially drawn to those who are in any way ignoring or neglecting their own self-care needs or who habitually put others first. They are often drawn to highly logical, analytical and 'heady' individuals for that reason. Many clients I've worked who have experienced narcissistic abuse are highly accomplished, productive, intelligent people, parents or professionals and have or have had successful careers or busy lives. Business owners, CEOs, directors, lawyers, therapists, nurses (or working in other caring or medical professions), investors, writers and managers… all very capable men and women. The focus throughout much of life has been about surviving, doing and achievement. Many people in relationships with a narcissist actually make wonderful project managers and trouble shooters. Typically they are the go-to people if you ever need anybody to get things done. However, they are a target for narcissists *because* of this busyness. People who are distracted and busy are too distracted to be vigilant to early signs of abuse. They are usually too concerned with trying to do whats right for others to speak up about how they really feel. Allied to that, sometimes victims of narcissistic abuse do not know enough about how they really feel, what they want or what their values are because of these traits. So in recovery, we turn the focus towards marking out time to know how we feel, to know what we want, to understand it's OK to state our needs and to speak up when we need to.

Whilst there may be lots of benefits to being some or all of the above to some extent, being so driven comes at a cost. When we are extremely goal or achievement focused or detached from our own self-care needs, we simultaneously push ourselves and tend to have a punitive or harsh inner self-talk. We neglect or ignore our *emotional* needs. It is the *do-er* who, despite experiencing grief, hurt or upset will defiantly insist *"I'm fine"*, *"It's fine"*, *"everything is fine"* and plough on regardless. So to survive and get through. They push away feelings, keep busy or endlessly distract themselves. This may not be conscious. They are often too busy to notice. Common distractions include simply being *busy-a-holics,* alcohol, drug-use, sex, shopping, workaholism, OCD or other obsessive, compulsive and addictive behaviours. Keeping busy or distracted, throwing yourself into work, parenting or family, having an endless 'to-do' list, being overly concerned as a carer, rescuer or fixer, or otherwise being more concerned with everybody else and attending to others needs instead of your own.

There is much in these ways of being that is highly attractive to a narcissist; the successes, money, prestige and status. But as well as these external qualities, it is ultimately a winning combination for a narcissist to find somebody who is somewhat disconnected from their own emotional needs and wants. One who will tend to comply and keep quiet. Somebody who is quick to be hard on themselves, to feel guilty, take responsibility or the blame – that is already helping the narcissist with what they intend you to do! Narcissists do not take responsibility for themselves so if you are quick to feel guilty or be hard on yourself you are an attractive proposition. By having a punitive relationship of any kind within yourself, you are going to make it easier for a narcissist to come along and reinforce that dynamic. Better still if you are somebody who, in whichever way, tends to neglect or ignore your own feelings, wants and needs – in favour of focusing on the narcissists – then even better for them. This is why it is absolutely crucial to address this imbalance *in yourself, for yourself* in order to guard and protect yourself from being a magnet to narcissists in the first place. This is an important part of moving on from toxic relationships.

When we are being too hard on ourselves, keeping too busy, engaging in unhealthy habits or lifestyle choices, working too much or too hard, focusing on other people or other things or other such behaviours and ways of being that are familiar to those in relationships with narcissists, we are probably ignoring or neglecting our own self-care needs. We are also potentially missing, to some extent, true and deep self-compassion.

True self-compassion is necessary to protect us from abusive situations and relationships. This needs some work in recovery

Needless to say, anybody who is actively taking really good care of themselves are much less likely to put up with abusive behaviour anyway.

Recovery is about developing a healthy relationship with yourself first and foremost. It's about healthy boundaries and self-care

Thriving comes from fundamentally having a loving, healthy relationship with yourself. One where you are kind and supportive to yourself. Where you allow yourself to do the things you enjoy and that are good for you. Make positive choices for yourself. Allow yourself to make mistakes. Don't take things too seriously. Allow yourself to see the positives. Know your self-worth and ultimately live an authentic, connected and fulfilling life. You can shift from survive and drive to thrive by becoming more aware of your own ways of being. This includes considering why you adopted these behaviours in the first place. Next it's developing self-care and self-compassion – working on the relationship you have with yourself. Learning to love and respect yourself. These are explored in further detail in following chapters.

Reflection point:

* Is it easier for me to focus on other peoples wants and needs?
* Can I recognise my own wants and needs? Do I respond to them appropriately?
* If not, why not?
* Do I keep myself too busy?
* Do I keep myself too distracted?
* Do I operate in survival mode? If so, how?
* How driven am I? Where has this drive or need for busyness come from?
* How has my ways of being served me in the past? Do they serve me now?
* What are the downsides?
* How has this way of being impacted on my health? Wellbeing? Self-care? Relationships?
* What kind of message does this give to other people? including children? partners? colleagues? friends?
* How often do I 'check-in' with myself and ask myself how I am?
* How am I right now?
* What might I need?
* What are my views about self-care?

* What are my views about:
    treating myself to something new or expensive.
    taking care of myself.
    taking time off.
    relaxing and resting
* Why?
* Is this harmful or healing to me and my recovery?
* Any further reflections?

12. Spotting the signs – Part 2 (It's an inside job)

The first part of learning how to 'spot the signs' in this book focused on the traits and actions of the *other*. However, another equally important part of learning how to spot the signs that we may be in contact with a narcissist is to sense within *ourselves* how *we feel on the inside*. What is happening inside of you right now? How does this person make you *feel* – emotionally, mentally, physically? How does *thinking* about this person or situation make you feel on the inside? What is your gut instinct telling you? What thoughts, feelings or physical sensations do you notice? What is that like? Just notice – these are signs.

Very often, people in abusive relationships have long disconnected to and stopped tuning into and most importantly *listening* to and *trusting* what is going on in the inside. We don't take heed of our instinct. We don't trust our inner wisdom and instead become paralysed at the receiving end of the narcissistic partners opinion. Quite like Echo, people here are in danger of losing their voice and in time, losing their sense of self.

I would like to explain more about this internal disconnect and mistrust as it is something that very much relates to destructive relationship patterns. Understanding and learning how to take notice of your internal compass can serve as a crucial narcissist detector and repellant for the future.

THE INTERNAL DISCONNECT BLOCKS THE SIGNS

One thing that has struck me in my clinical work in the area of narcissistic abuse is how analytical, logical and 'heady' people tend to be who are or have been involved in abusive relationships with narcissists. This is a risky way to operate in relationships because if we are too analytical, too much of the time, we are in serious danger of missing our inner felt sense. The part of us that instinctively senses something is wrong. Instead we rely on our logic – but logic does not work with narcissism. The actions and behaviours of a narcissist are impossible to understand with logic. Logic is simply the wrong tool for the job. If we are too in our heads, too intellectual or analytical and not in touch enough with our emotional landscape then we are in serious danger of missing out on the important warning signs that our instincts are there to give us. It is our bodies, our emotions, our gut instinct and felt sense that we can learn to trust and rely on. Too often though, for whatever reason, those attracted to and importantly, attractive *to* narcissists are those who are somewhat disconnected to their inner knowing. It makes sense doesn't it? If you are highly in tune with your emotional experience, your feelings and your gut – and trusting and confident in that – then you are going to be more in touch with your values, your likes, dislikes, wants and needs. You will automatically be in tune with your boundaries – what's OK and not OK for you. Anything that goes against your inner compass would absolutely not sit right at all. You would feel more confident and more OK with speaking up and saying *"this is not OK for me"*, *"I don't like it"*, *"I deserve better"*. With being fully integrated in mind, body, thoughts, emotions and instinctive self, you quite naturally protect yourself from being prey to abusive narcissists. This has been the basis of my own recovery from narcissistic abuse.

Narcissists will seek to be around people who are, to varying degrees, disconnected to their own feelings, beliefs, wants and needs. This is because people are much easier to manipulate and control when they are not connected. Narcissistic abuse in its essence is about the narcissist seeking and attempting in whichever way they can to create a relationship dynamic where the other gives up their own wants, needs and feelings in order to serve the narcissists. It is much easier for a narcissist to mould the focus to be about themselves with somebody who is not focusing or taking enough notice of their own feelings or instincts already. It's an ideal starting place. Do not hand this on a plate to them! Do not make this easy for them. I strongly suggest a key fundamental in recovery is to really learn how to connect and fully integrate all parts within *you*. This is an inside job. This forms a strong shield of protection against narcissists and is also key to developing and maintaining a firm sense of boundaries, self-esteem and self-worth – all of which are interrelated.

I have studied the mind over a long period of time and to a high level to come to the clear conclusion that the mind is where the problems exist. It is not always however, where the solutions lie. I believe this especially true when it comes to recovery from narcissistic abuse. More often than not, those who have been subjected to narcissistic abuse have either made excuses for, or justified the rationale for why they have put up with unacceptable behaviour. Or created distress for themselves by trying to understand a narcissists wide range of terrible and cruel actions with logic.

Narcissists are illogical. Their contradictory behaviour is illogical. You cannot apply logic to illogical people and behaviour

I am personally a firm believer that our minds will tell us all sorts of nonsense – because quite frankly, that is what our minds do! However, it is essential to remember that: *thoughts are not facts*.

Our bodies on the other hand, in my opinion, do not and cannot lie. Our bodies hold a deeper sense of knowing. It is a case of learning how to tune in and understand that language and develop a mind-body communication. We all have an intrinsic inner wisdom we can trust. We have emotions and a gut instinct for a reason. They indicate important signs and communicate ongoing feedback to us. It's a fundamental part of our primitive survival instinct that has done its job for centuries. We are all here because of it. You can trust and rely on that inner wisdom to help guide to what is best for you. You can use this to sense into more of what you really *need*. In order to hear that communication though, you must learn how to connect, tune into and listen to it. If necessary, take the time from now to build total trust in it. Trust comes in time.

The notion of tuning into this inner knowing, that is separate to our analytically thinking mind, is a key part of mind-body based approaches. It's feeling the body with the body. It can take a bit of work in the beginning though, especially if you are not so used to it. The practice of this reconnection and communication can be developed through mind-body approaches like mindfulness and insight awareness practice. Other mind-body practises can also help such as yoga, meditation, tai chi, martial arts and some aspects of spiritual practice including prayer and connecting to a higher power. The main thing is to give yourself the space and time to check in with yourself. To switch off distractions, quieten the mind, slow down and be still enough to listen and notice to what is happening on the inside.

FURTHER EXPLORING THE DISCONNECT

It is not uncommon in our modern, fast-paced world to see that we have stopped tuning in, listening to or trusting our internal sense. This is hardly a surprise. In our culture, we are not readily encouraged to develop this communication. This is not something we learn in school or at work. In fact, I think more often than not, the emphasis all round is to ignore our inner world. We are encouraged instead to focus on the external world and on endless distractions. We push ourselves, distract or change how we feel. This is in part why there is an epidemic of stress, depression and burn out. Aversion to or changing how we feel is the basis of what any addiction serves. Any addiction, regardless of drug of choice, be it; alcohol, gambling, sex, love, work, compulsive care-taking… all serve to either keep us away from our feelings or to change how we feel. The problem then is not so much the addiction, but more so our reluctance and resistance to feel whatever it is we feel. This is modern day madness. We have feelings for a reason. Our emotions are our internal compass. We need not be scared of them. On the contrary, we can trust them.

Being too busy, resistant or too distracted to know what you are feeling is a problem when it comes to narcissistic abuse.

Whilst you remain disconnected and distracted from the layers of your own inner emotional landscape you remain attractive to a narcissist. Narcissists tend not to go too near people who are in touch with and stay close to their values or who affirm how they feel. Those who honour their inner wisdom and whom have the courage and strength to stay strong and loyal to it, repel narcissists. This is because when you are truly in touch with how you feel, and are able to trust your instincts and respond to your feelings appropriately, you are more likely to notice and communicate when things do not feel OK. You are more likely to say 'NO'. Being in touch is linked to boundaries. Boundaries come from being in tune with your values and what feels OK or not OK for you. Boundaries come from knowing what is acceptable and what is not, what you want and what you don't want. Boundaries are intrinsically linked to self-worth and self-esteem. Narcissists have issues with boundaries. They do not like healthy boundaries and tend to stay away from people with them.

WHY DO WE DISCONNECT?

So society generally speaking does not encourage a vast amount of space for self-reflection or self-awareness. We were not always like that though. When we are born we are very much in direct contact with our feelings, our pain and hunger, our wants and needs. We communicated that in a very direct way – we screamed and cried to get what we wanted. We are in touch with our felt sense before we even learn the use of language and certainly before we learn the use of cognitive, analytical and logical thinking. It is quite normal then to learn to pay more attention to thoughts or external goings on than our inner sense or feelings. It may have even benefited us growing up to attune to other peoples feelings and moods over our own. Maybe that helped us survive our family home or school. Another thing that can happen that facilitates disconnect between mind and body is if somewhere along the line you have learnt that it is not safe to be in touch or stay with how you are feeling. Perhaps the feelings at particular moments growing up were too overwhelming. This often happens if we have experienced something that has been too frightening, too scary, too unpleasant or too confusing. This disconnect is what happens when we experience trauma. When our experience in any particular moment is too much, too shocking or sudden or too overwhelming for our brains to be able to process properly at that time, we can be left feeling quite 'disconnected'.

Some of us were never encouraged to trust our own sense of what we felt, or what we wanted in the first place. This can happen during childhood if the adults around us for whatever reason haven't acknowledged, allowed us or supported us to embrace our own internal experience. Instead, our internal and emotional experience is negated by the adults around us and we learn to ignore or not trust it. For example, feeling frightened as a youngster but having an adult or other people dismissing your experience or telling you that's not the case *"oh don't be silly, of course you're not scared!"* This may not seem significant but if we experience enough of this kind of feedback it becomes incredibly confusing for any child or young person. They are left confused and unsure about their emotions and feelings. *"I thought I was scared... but mum is telling me I'm not... I guess I'm not? In fact I'm not even sure what I feel anymore..."* and so they learn not to trust their internal experience or signals. Ideally parents attune, recognise and acknowledge the feelings of the child. When this has not occurred it can lead to disconnect – it's too difficult to do anything else. It's a way we learn to survive. Conflicting feedback growing up leaves us feeling confused, mistrusting and hopeless.

Another example of being taught to go against our inner knowing is a typical childhood experience of being pushed to do something you don't really want to do. *"I really don't want to kiss Granny – she has a moustache and smells a bit funny"* thinks

Simon aged six. His instinct is sensing it's something he would rather not do. However, unfortunately our internal experience as children is often overridden by the rules and instructions of the adults around us – that is the nature of childhood. *"Don't be rude, come on, you know you kiss Granny goodbye when we leave..."* And so he does. Again, enough of these kinds of experiences are enough to learn that our feelings do not matter. That we should go against what we want or that we should not take notice of our internal sense that may be telling us something does not feel right. We can easily learn as children how to go against what our inner sense is telling us. We learn to ignore what we want and instead we learn what to do in order to please others, despite it not feeling nice for us. We neglect our needs or wants in favour of doing what is 'right'. Except it's not.

As previously mentioned, sometimes we learn to cut off from trusting or listening to our inner experience because at some point it was too unpleasant or overwhelming to stay in touch with. That is when a disconnect serves a helpful function. If the feelings were too scary or horrible, then it is helpful that we disconnect from that. That is a primitive survival instinct. Perhaps the arguments at home were too disturbing, dads drinking was too violent and unpredictable. Mums anxiety was too much, our brothers mood swings too intolerable. Maybe the bullying at school was too horrid. Perhaps we have not been encouraged, shown or supported to develop trust in our inner knowing – it's not something we learn on the curriculum! Remember, that disconnect can serve a helpful function at that time. It may have helped you get through school or a difficult home situation. However, it is not a healthy long-term way of being. Crucially this can also be a magnet for narcissists and other toxic relationships. If we ignore and disregard our feelings and wants then we make ourselves prime target for bullies to come along and take advantage.

Whatever your past experiences, whether it is to do with growing up, trauma or just how you are for whatever reason, you have most likely lost some inner connection and trust in that. I often hear clients describe a battle between gut instinct and mind. This could be a key part of what interferes with your ability to do what is right for *you*; whether that be to hold a boundary, to self-care, to say 'no', or to end things and walk away.

"I knew he lied to me, I knew he was cheating, I felt it. I had seen the evidence. I'd read the texts and emails. He denied it. He told me I was imagining things, that I was jealous, possessive and that I was going mad. My gut instinct and my body was telling me to run, to get out, that I deserved better, but at the same time I felt paralysed by fear. I kept thinking; 'but he's saying it's me and maybe it is? Maybe I got it wrong? Maybe he will change, he says he wants to make it work'. I wanted to believe that. In my mind I could make up all sorts of excuses and justifications as to why I should stay, as to how things were going to be better, but in retrospect I can see I was sick. My gut was screaming at me to go, but I overrode my felt-sense with the logical, rational voice in my head that told me that I should be a good girl and stay and make it OK. It was complete denial. The decisions made from my head were wrong but when I eventually listened to my gut instinct it was so clear. I knew I had to go, I knew I'd had enough. The sense in my body, that I had ignored for so long, was certain. After years of emotional abuse and of feeling worthless, not good enough, anxious and fearful I just got to the point where I felt deep down, something had to change. After one particularly bad argument and him then trying to make me feel like I was to blame, I suddenly could see it all more clearly. I had reached my limit. I packed my things and left. To be honest, the first few months after I left was excruciating. I was obsessed with him. I played the whole relationship through my mind again and again, desperately trying to work it out. It was mental torture. I would feel anxious and tearful one minute, feel completely

guilty and feel like I'd got it all wrong. Then be overcome with rage and anger the next, but I just rode out the feelings. It got easier in time.

I was able to focus more on myself and less on him and that was really when things started to change for me. I was quite shocked as to how habitual it was for me to be obsessing about him, his feelings, his wants or likes and nothing for myself. With practise and a lot of conscious effort I really found myself again. I spend time checking-in with myself everyday, asking myself how I am, how I am feeling, physically, emotionally, sensing into what I need. It was quite strange at the beginning and quite a shock to realise I had never really done that before. I always knew how everybody else was – yet I had no gauge on myself, not really. I had to put the effort in. It took work and practice but in time I discovered how to care better for myself, how to recognise what I was feeling, what I needed and to give myself that. I've learnt to trust myself and to trust my instinct. It is much more reliable than the crazy ideas my head can tell me! Like all the times it said; "Go back, it will be fine". It was madness. I knew in my gut it was never going to be. Now I know I can trust that. It's my internal alarm system and I notice it more and more. I could never and will never go against it again."

To summarise, when we have earlier experiences of overwhelm, regardless of how big or small or seemingly insignificant, we can experience some disconnect between mind and body. The sorts of experience I am referring to here are earlier traumas, accidents, or bullying, sibling rivalry, grief and loss, or frightening situations like arguments, fights, being attacked, burgled or generally times of feeling scared or insecure. It can happen no matter how big or small these incidents may seem. It may also include times when the adults around at that time were, for whatever reason, unable to provide the comfort, reassurance or encouragement we needed as a child. We sometimes learn to disconnect as a survival instinct because sometimes it's safer to. This disconnect can also be modelled and encouraged in families who are emotionally disconnected themselves. Usually they tend to be more focused on intellect, achievement and drive, material success or status, rather than compassion or honouring and encouraging emotional development. Culturally we tend to be more readily rewarded for being 'heady', analytical, cognitive, mentally and intellectually driven. Being more in our heads and less in our bodies comes at a price and simultaneously distances us from our emotional experience. Being disconnected from our emotional experience can sometimes be wrongly and dangerously interpreted as being 'strong'. I've worked with many people who have ended up in abusive narcissist relationships as adults who grew up with family messages of: *'be strong'*, *'suck it up and get on with it'*, *'that's life'*, *'deal with it'*, *'it's fine, you're fine, we're all fine (when we are not)'*. These kinds of messages all communicate and encourage a dismissing of your inner emotional experience.

There are gains to be had from adopting a more disconnected way of being. As previously mentioned, some of this can be about emotional survival for a period of time. It's how many people achieve, succeed and get things done. Sometimes it is necessary to get to where we want to be in life or to get through difficult times. However, staying in this kind of disconnect full-time, long-term or being stuck in intellect or logic is commonplace in people who find themselves in abusive relationships. So in recovery, this should be considered and addressed by practising mindfulness, insight development and grounding techniques to support contact with the emotional parts of our being.

DEVELOPING A (RE)CONNECTION

Many people I have worked with report that in hindsight, they recognise they actually had a nagging gut feeling or sense that this person wasn't right, wasn't being honest, wasn't good for them, were not trustworthy and so on. However, with such a heavy over-reliance on the analytical mind they chose to listen to the justifying and excuse-making mind – rather than their instinct or the range of vital somatic signs from the body. I think a lot of us are guilty of this. I know I have been in the past. It's very much what we learn in our culture, family and education system. We are rarely taught how to pay mindful attention to what's happening in our bodies, our guts, our sense of our heart. If we have never been taught how to do this, then simply we never learn how to do it. This though makes us vulnerable and attractive to narcissists. We live in an age where this sensing into ourselves in an integrated way is largely discouraged. We are rewarded to rely upon our heads, our intellect, our cognitive reasoning more than anything else. If growing up was emotionally painful, then coming up into our heads and focusing on academia, logic or intellect serves an important and useful function of keeping us away from our feelings. When our feelings are too unpleasant this is helpful. However it is not a healthy long-term solution. When it comes to working through patterns of abusive relationships as well as in recovering from narcissistic abuse:

Learning how to tune into, listen and hear what the body, heart and gut instinct are communicating to you is an essential part of recovery

It can be helpful to embrace and engage with any kind of mindful or reflective practices such as meditation, yoga or tai chi to help establish or re-establish a dialogue between mind and body. Quiet insight and reflection can help. We may have to learn the difference between the mind, thoughts and feelings. This can take time. Working with a therapist may help with this.

Spotting the signs from the inside is a protective factor in any further abuse. I have seen many people meet a narcissist and in the early stages become instantly swept away in the romance and fantasy of it all. They allow the love-bombing to completely cloud any judgement of their own and totally lose perspective. Sorry to be the bearer of bad news here, but in reality, relationships are simply not like they are in the movies. As quick as a narcissist will claim to fall head over heels in love with you is as quick as they will fall out of love again or move onto the next. Narcissistic romance is powerful and can leave you thinking like you have met *'the one'* or that you share a *'divine special connection'*. A narcissist will obviously encourage this and likely say things in various ways such as:

"Nobody else can make me feel like this!"

"Nobody understands me or makes me laugh like you do!"

"I've never felt a connection like this before"

These could be signs of narcissism and potentially the beginnings of an unhealthy relationship. They are also signs of love-bombing – a technique any narcissist will use to overwhelm and woo potential partners during the early stages of a relationship. Sure, we may want to believe this to be true, however, healthy relationships take time to grow. It takes many years to truly get to know somebody. Healthy relationships involve negotiation, compromise, healthy boundaries, interdependence, understanding and mutual respect. It is important to slow down, stay grounded and take time to feel into the experience. If it feels too good to be true – that's usually because it is.

NOTICING THE SIGNS FROM THE INSIDE

If you have already experienced the end of a relationship with a narcissist you may have been left feeling like you never really knew them. Many, many people are left in a state of shock and disbelief after experiencing narcissistic abuse. A strange sense of feeling quite confused about what you ever had in common, or who they really were. Many people are left feeling like they never really knew and may never know. Healing from narcissistic abuse requires letting go of the any need to know. After narcissistic abuse you will be left with several unanswered questions. Instead of relying on logic to try to work out the answers (which in itself will feel maddening) you in time will find it more helpful to instead sit with the feelings and then attend to your needs in response to that. And let go of the need to know, control or make anything happen.

Narcissists are quite the chameleon. You can avoid repeating patterns and getting pulled into a relationship with a narcissist or even being pulled into a relationship again too soon, by finding ways to stay grounded and centred in yourself. Narcissists tend to appear when we are at our most vulnerable. I have seen many people come out of a relationship with a narcissist only to jump straight back into another one. Give yourself proper time to heal. Narcissists will arrive to rescue like a knight in shining armour when we are most unsuspecting. Stay vigilant. Remember, any abuser will want to destabilise a potential victim. It is how they gain control and power. A narcissist will seek to destabilise others in a number of ways; usually in the beginnings this is done through charm, bombarding with compliments, gifts, rescuing, controlling, affection and attention. Destabilising is also achieved through more abusive ways, as is seen a bit further on into the relationship.

Stay vigilant to spotting the signs both in what you are observing externally as well as what you are feeling on the inside

It is important to honestly consider: *Is this person a little too charming? What does it feel like? Does it feel 'too much too soon'? Does it feel a bit too good to be true? Am I anxious when in communication with them? Does this feel a bit manic? Do I feel anxious if I don't hear from them? Is it worryingly powerful or overwhelming? Does it feel too intense?* Remember intensity is not the same as intimacy. If the answer to any of these questions is any hint of a yes, it's possibly a warning sign. Trust your inner feeling and sense of knowing. It tends to be much more reliable than our changeable, unhelpful and sometimes inaccurate thinking!

Other questions to consider include:

* *How do I feel when I think about or when I'm with this person?*
* *What is my gut instinct telling me about this person or situation?*
* *Do they talk about themselves a lot? Do they ask me questions? What is it like when I'm talking?*
* *Do I find that I retreat, quieten or comply?*
* *Is this exciting or scary? Maybe a bit of both?*
* *What would good friends or family think or say?*
* *Does this person seem genuinely interested in me? Are they attentive?*
* *What is their relationship or family history? What are their friends like?*
* *How do I feel when I am with them?*
* *What would I be sensing if this was happening to a good friend or if I was watching this from a distance?*
* *Do I feel free to be totally myself with this person?*
* *Am I relaxed?*
* *Do I feel tense?*
* *Does it feel exciting or intense? Could this be a warning sign?*
* *Do I feel oppressed? Suffocated?*
* *Do I feel like I lose my voice when this person is around?*
* *Am I idolised by them? Does it feel too much?*

* *Is there a sense of freezing, tension or tightness in my body at all when I'm with this person?*
* *What do I notice happens on the inside when I am with them?*
* *How do I feel after spending time with them?*
* *What is it like for me when I hear from /don't hear from this person?*
* *What could these physical or emotional feelings or sensations be telling me?*
* *What do I need right now that is a loving, caring thing that I can give myself?*

There are no right or wrong answers... it's more important to just tune in and notice what the answers are for yourself.

GROWING TOWARD SELF-CONNECTION AND SELF-CARE

It is important to find ways to give yourself space and time and to help you stay grounded and centred in order to best assess and gauge your instinct. Some mindfulness and grounding techniques are covered in an earlier chapter. Speaking to friends, family, colleagues or a professional can also help you to retain a healthy and helpful perspective. When in interaction with others, try to stay tuned into your own experience and to take your time. Try to keep the focus on you and within you. If meeting somebody new, if things are good and it feels right, then all the more reason to go slowly and really savour the exploration and enjoy getting to know each other. It may be difficult in the beginning to tell the difference between what your mind is telling you and in noticing the nuance of messages in the body. Be patient. It takes time. It comes with practice. Developing this reconnection is already deepening your self-care.

Space for self-reflection and self-connection – A Daily Practice:
This practice is developed by setting time aside each day to give ourselves the space to sit quietly, away from any distractions, to simply reflect and ask ourselves:

"How am I today?",
"How am I right now?"
"What do I need, that I can give myself,
that is a loving thing for me?"

How often do you ask yourself how you are? This question is especially important for anybody who relates to traits or characteristics of codependency or echoism. If this is you, you are probably so used to knowing and being more concerned with how everybody else is, and what everybody else needs, that you have lost touch with yourself in this way. I recognise this in my clinical work when I might ask a client how they are and they reply by telling me how somebody else is, perhaps how the narcissist in their life might be doing or feeling. That is not the question. The focus is about you. Now is the time, if you haven't already done so, to *really* learn how to tune into *yourself*. This is about self-care; checking in with yourself; "How am I?" Take some quiet time each day to ask yourself these questions. Either mentally or use a journal. Carving out space for regular and ongoing check-ins, quiet contemplation and self-reflection is not only helpful for recovery from narcissistic abuse but is a fundamental in self-care and in building a healthy relationship within yourself. Checking in with others and sharing how you feel is equally important. Reach out to friends or people in your support network for the opportunity to share this with each other and to develop more healthy connections.

Healthy relationships start with the
one we have with ourselves.
Get to know and care for you.

Exercise:

*Finding a quiet, comfortable space, at a time you won't be
disturbed or distracted, take a few minutes to sense into
where you are sitting or lying. Take some time to just notice,
through all of your senses, what you can physically feel on
the outside of your body... the coldness of the floor, or the
support of the chair on your legs, buttocks, back. Just notice
how warm or cold that feels right now. Notice any sounds
coming from around you or from outside. Not to allow them
to be distractions, but to just notice. Are there any smells at
all? What do you notice?*

*Then gently bring your attention to the breath for a while.
Just noticing how you are breathing right now. No need to judge
or try to control or change the breathing at all – just notice
the natural inhalations and exhalations. You may even like to
incorporate a 'mindfulness of breath' practice where at the end
of each exhalation you count, continuing until you reach 10
exhalations and then simply continue by beginning again at 1.
Gently quietening and focusing the mind.*

*After you have spent a few minutes arriving a little more into
the present moment and tuning into your surroundings, your
sensations and breath, then take some time to gently tune into
what's happening on the inside. How are you feeling? How are
you feeling right now? It can be helpful to mentally do a body
scan, starting from the head, slowly working through each body
part to just check in and ask "What's that like there right now?".*

*So starting with the head and the mind, asking yourself,
"What's that like right now?" And finding fitting labels for your
direct experience. Is the head and the mind still feeling full of the
day? Buzzy? Fizzy? Calm? Anxious? Resistant?*

Continuing slowly and gently moving your attention down through the body to spend time with each part of your physical self, checking in as to how it is right now? Tense? Relaxed? Aching? Discomfort? A sense of ease? Peace? Apprehension? Neutral? Whatever it might be... pay close attention and just notice how this exploration unfolds.

Working from the head, slowly guide your mental attention down through the face, the jaw, the neck, shoulders, arms, chest, back, abdomen, hips, buttocks, thighs, knees, calves, ankles and feet. There are no right or wrongs. We are not looking to make anything happen, just notice. Just notice what is, right now, in this moment.

Once you have worked through the body scan, then it's time to gently turn your attention to your emotional experience. You may not notice much. It may be subtle. It may be that not much is happening right now. You may feel a surge of feelings. It may be fear arising, anxiety, sadness, a sense of loss. Anger. Whatever it is just notice. Just notice what is there and what it's like.

So for example, you may notice a feeling. There may be a mixture of feelings. Just notice what is there in the body, trying if you can, to resist the urge to come up into the head to work it out, to analyse or change anything. No need to change anything, just notice. If you notice a tendency to come up into the thinking, then just notice that too. What was the urge? What did you notice? What did that feel like? Trying to stay with and sense into what is happening right now, in this moment. If you identify emotions, try to notice how you recognise them. How do you know you feel what you feel? Are there any bodily sensations that go with that? What's happening to the breath right now? How do the neck and shoulders feel? How does the tummy feel? Just notice...

If you can, try to practice this on a regular basis and as you sit through this practice for 10-15 minutes, noticing the natural unfolding of this experience, you may arrive at tuning into a sense of what you might need for yourself right now? Having *stilled and quietened yourself enough to be a little more in touch with what's going on for you right now, gently ask yourself "How am I today? How am I right now?" Wait for the answers to arise. Your inner wisdom will respond in time. And to close with, you can then ask yourself "What is it that I need? What can I do for myself right now that is kind and loving?". Just notice. Listen. And respond by then caring for yourself in whichever way you feel you need right now.*

DAILY CHECK-IN:

Ask yourself on a regular basis *"How am I?"*, *"How am I feeling right now?"* Acknowledge and label any feelings. Acknowledge and name any physical sensations. Watch what happens next. Having acknowledged feelings and/or physical sensations ask yourself *"What do I need?"*, *"What can I do for myself right now that is healthy and loving for me?"*.

By the nature of narcissistic abuse, the focus tends to be on the narcissist, because it's all about them, all of the time. Being disconnected or readily willing and able to neglect your own feelings or needs in favour of focusing on somebody else is magnetic for a narcissist. This usually only continues more and more into the relationship and adds to the abuse and trauma. So you will see that already recovery is very much about bringing the focus back to yourself for now. Not in a selfish or narcissistic way, but the focus needs to be on you, and away from the narcissist.

It is very typical to feel trapped at the stage of trying to work it all out, to understand why the narcissist has done what they have done and how it all happened. This can feel completely maddening. You may well have a whole host of questions that you want answers for. It is perfectly understandable as we try to make sense of our experience with logic. However, with narcissistic abuse we will often have questions that we will never get answers to. It becomes then more important to let go of the need to know. Let go of the need to make sense or to turn the clock back, or to justify, to explain or to say something, to understand, to change them, to control them or to make things different. It is futile and enough to leave you feeling like you are going insane. It will keep you stuck. Instead accept that there may well be unanswered questions. That said, focus then on yourself, on what you are doing, how you are feeling and what you need right now. It needs to be about you for now in order to be able to return to some healthy balance in time. The following is a 4-step technique to help you to check out where your attention is and if necessary, return it to you in a kind and supportive way. I would encourage you to try to use this as much as possible, especially in the early stages of recovery from narcissistic abuse or other toxic relationships.

4-PART STEP PROCESS TO HELP BRING THE FOCUS BACK TO YOU:

1. Recognise where your thoughts and attentions are. Ask yourself 'What am I thinking about?' Notice. Mindfulness of thoughts practice can help with this.
2. If you recognise your thoughts and attention are on the narcissist or on trying to understand or work it all out, gently acknowledge that to yourself in a compassionate and non-judgemental way.
3. Gently bring the focus back to yourself by asking yourself 'How do I feel right now?' 'What is going on for me in this moment?' It is likely that there are thoughts or feelings inside of you that may have led to you focusing elsewhere so now we want to gently bring our focus back to what really needs our attention. Ask yourself 'What do I notice about what is going on for _me_ right now?' Are there any thoughts, feelings,

emotions, physical sensations, memories or images? Do I have any urges? Try to just notice what is happening. Try to calmly, gently and compassionately stay in touch with this for a moment or two to just give this some space. Let whatever there is come up and out. Label whatever it is you notice.

4. Having noticed and named any thoughts, feelings or sensations then ask yourself what it is <u>you</u> need in this moment, that is kind and loving for you? It may be to give yourself permission to feel whatever it is you are feeling. It may be to take good care of yourself, get some rest, eat well, reach out to a friend, take a bath, watch a film, read a book, run, scream, cry, do nothing. Whatever it is you feel that you need, that is **healthy and healing for you and your recovery**, then gift yourself that.

This is how we start to re-focus back to ourselves. This practice helps us to get to know ourselves, to develop kindness, understanding, forgiveness and compassion and also importantly teaches us how to self-care. Most people with codependency issues or a pattern of being in relationships with narcissists are really skilled at caring for everyone else. Now it is time to fine tune those skills to YOU. It's an inside job.

13. The Process of Recovery

In the first instance, it is quite something to have suspicions and indeed come to the realisation you may be in a relationship with a narcissist. Arming yourself with information about narcissism, why people develop such personalities or traits and how to spot the signs are an important and necessary first step. This is a stage when the lens in which you view this person/or people may alter. You may notice more and begin to view patterns of behaviour in a different way. The focus and perspective becomes clearer. For many people, this is a hugely enlightening stage. I have witnessed many times a helpful shift the right kind of information and understanding can offer. It can be the knowledge and awareness that helps move somebody from chronically feeling like it's them and their fault to beginning to regain a healthier balance and perspective. This stage can also very much feel like the lid has been taken off a previously very confusing and maddening situation. Once a light illuminates our experience, and we 'see', it is thankfully very difficult to then fall back and 'unsee'. This is what comes with awareness and awareness is key to change.

With narcissistic abuse a number of issues usually already exist that play a part in why we might find ourselves in an abusive relationship in the first place. These include:

* Childhood experiences of narcissism / Narcissistic parent/s. Addicted parent/s and/or issues of codependency in the family
* Self-neglect/care issues
* Over-achievement / too achievement-focused
* Distracted / Disconnected
* A need to caretake or rescue others
* Difficulty with healthy boundaries
* Too much focus on others wants and needs
* Not enough focus on your own
* Issues of anxiety, fear, guilt or shame or unresolved trauma

During an abusive relationship several things can be affected or destroyed; our self-esteem, self-worth, self-belief, self-care, confidence, trust, our values, boundaries, communication issues as well as associated trauma from any of the above. Working on these aspects then form the recipe for recovery. Each of these areas and more are explored in further detail in following chapters.

At this stage however, I would like to share a point about the usefulness of *slowing down...* and really absorbing and considering what is discussed and suggested in each chapter. It's very, very easy, especially when we are bright and our minds are racing (as is so often the case when we are fresh from narcissistic abuse) to skim through the reading and skip past points, because we easily already know and 'get the gist' or are keen to move on. However, there is a real danger of skimming the theory and missing the benefits of the practice if we do this. This can slow and negatively impact on recovery from narcissistic abuse further down the road. So at this stage, I would really like to encourage you to slow down and spend some time reflecting on parts of the reading and on anything else you might be learning or realising. It is easy and dangerous for example, to skip past the section on self-talk and declare it's not so relevant, or *'I'm OK with my self-talk'*, *'I don't need to do that'*, or *'yep, I get it'*. Please slow down for yourself, reflect and put these ideas into practice. There is almost always room for more insight, awareness and growth.

This book is written in a way that is designed to build on each layer, starting with the groundwork and foundations. As with any build, the foundations are crucial. If the foundations are not in place properly from the beginning, then at a later stage, what you add on top is not supported or steady and can come crashing down. Please don't rush and then find yourself stuck at a later stage because of racing ahead without it connecting. Try to take your time and build solid foundations, whilst continuing to steadily move forward. Be patient. Work on each point and build the layers, slowly but surely. This supports a more effective and speedier recovery in the long run.

Recovery begins when you turn the focus to yourself. Whilst coming to realisations about abusive and narcissistic relationships can ultimately be a positive thing for change and growth, it can also be a difficult, confusing and challenging stage. We can become stuck at the stage of desperately trying to work out and intellectually make sense of our experience. We can get stuck at trying to understand the narcissist. This is just another form of too much focus being on the narcissist. This is the issue in the first place. This is where and when focusing and learning to take good care of yourself becomes truly essential. Self-care is a priority for now. True self care is about really becoming your own best friend. It's being a loving, patient and supporting partner to yourself.

LAYING THE FOUNDATIONS FOR RECOVERY – SELF-CARE

Self-care is a vital fundamental in recovery from narcissistic abuse. Usually this is something that has been neglected or lost along the way before or during a toxic relationship. Often we are accustomed to focusing our care efforts on other people. In recovery now, it is essential that you learn how to take care of yourself first and foremost. You are responsible for your self-care. At early stages of recovery, self-care can simply mean making sure you eat well today, to get out or reach out to people for support. Further honing your self-care and self-soothing skills is important. Crucially, it helps reconnect us with our values. Self-care can help you to discover or remember what you like or enjoy and what is important to you. This is stuff that can get lost in an abusive relationship but importantly is a key part of recovery. Learning about what you like and doing more of what you enjoy is a vital part of building self-esteem as well as developing healthy boundaries which will be discussed later.

For now, think about ways you can practice and develop self-care. Some suggestions include:

* Begin each day with a positive affirmation
* Eat well
* Spend time in nature
* Treat yourself to a nice gift; a new coat, shoes or a nice meal
* Spend time with positive people, people who have your best interests at heart
* Get a manicure or haircut
* Allow yourself rest
* Read or watch positive literature or programmes
* Book a spa day or massage
* Try to live within each day – 24 hour living
* Practice mindfulness
* Exercise
* Be kind to yourself
* Embrace your quirks and qualities
* Laugh. Watch a funny movie or go see a stand-up comedian
* Visit a friend or relative who you enjoy spending time with
* Join a club

* Have some abstinence from alcohol/sugar/caffeine
* Learn something new
* Pick up a new hobby or an old interest that you've let slip
* Don't be hard on yourself
* Develop the ability to laugh at yourself sometimes
* Recognise and name your positive attributes
* Meditate
* Practice yoga
* Take a break or vacation
* Read a book
* Say nice things to yourself
* Compliment yourself / congratulate yourself
* Identify what brings you joy and makes you happy
* Do more of what brings you joy and makes you happy
* Remember thoughts aren't facts!
* Give yourself permission to do what feels right for you
* Be patient
* Forgive yourself and others
* Set aside time each week for a digital detox
* Pray
* Enjoy a long, hot bath
* Spend regular time just for relaxing
* Go for a walk or jog
* Visit a gallery, exhibition, theatre or cinema – book tickets for something you would like to see
* Try to let go of guilt and shame
* Be grateful – write a gratitude list at the end of each day

Being kind to yourself and good self-care absolutely includes doing a wide range of nice things for yourself. Taking time out to relax, treating yourself well, booking spa treatments, massage, reflexology, gym, swimming, yoga, relaxing with friends, travelling, treating yourself to nice gifts, manicures, new shoes, or anything else you like. Try to really get to know what you like and enjoy. It is a great practice to become more conscious and active with your self-care practices.

Hobbies & Interests

Many people affected by abusive and narcissistic relationships report a sense of having lost themselves. The focus over time has become more and more about the narcissist and all that they want or like. In the meantime echo shrinks and starts to lose her voice. You may find you have lived for some time in more of a drive and survive mode in opposed to thrive and enjoying life. Now is the time to consider and perhaps rediscover your passions and interests. What do you enjoy? What do you like doing? What hobbies or interests have you lost over time? How would you like to spend your time? What is a perfect day or weekend for you? Is there anything at all you have always wanted to try or learn but haven't yet? What might you like to do? Are there any classes or groups you'd like to join? Anywhere you'd like to visit? Any show or artist you'd like to see? What kinds of things do you enjoy?

This can be absolutely anything. As an idea, it may be related to: health and fitness, animal welfare, travel, cookery, theatre and arts, crafts, volunteer work, support groups, support work, holistic therapies, golf, yoga, running, climbing, biking, sightseeing, going some place new, writing, reading, new course, academic studies, just for fun... Anything and everything. Grant yourself permission to explore and discover.

Social Support & Connection

Having a healthy support network of people you can talk to, enjoy being with and can share experiences with is vital for our wellbeing at any time. Human connection is essential for our wellbeing. It is especially important in recovery from narcissistic abuse. Often partners, particularly of narcissists, may have found they have slowly lost interest in going out, in seeing or speaking to friends, family or colleagues during the relationship. This is often encouraged by the abuser as they want to pull you away from those with your best interests at heart and instead isolate you. People are much easier to control and manipulate when they are on their own. Now is the time to reach out and further develop, reestablish or begin to develop a strong and supportive network. This can be done by reaching out to friends old or new, family or colleagues and talking to them about what has been or is going on for you. Share with people what it is you need. Do not be afraid to ask for help. Despite the fears that may go with that, more times than not, reaching out is met with appreciation, understanding, respect and relief by others. Real friends will be there for you. I cannot recount the amount of times clients I have worked with have reached out to other people, others mothers at school, colleagues or neighbours and by doing so have actually helped somebody else come to realise issues in their own life. Or they may be going through something similar and it has been powerful to hear somebody else talk to them who understands. It works both ways. If this is not available for you, reach out to find support. Find a therapist you can talk to. There are support groups you can join or 12 step meetings may be applicable. Joining groups of like-minded people with similar interests can be a great way to meet people and make friends. Being subject to narcissistic abuse can be incredibly isolating and leave you feeling like it's *"my fault"* or *"I'm a failure"*, which can get in the way of reaching out and speaking out. It is important that you do though. One thing that strikes many, many of the clients I work with is how wide-spread this kind of experience is. It takes the courage to talk to somebody else about it to find that they know something about it, perhaps even having experienced it themselves. It is so important to talk about. Not least so you gain support for yourself but also to help raise important discussions and awareness.

Be specific, realistic and set yourself a timescale to make enquiries and get started with something. Enjoy it. This is your time to discover or rediscover yourself, your values, passions and interests. Notice how it feels to do more of what is right or good for you. Spend more time with people that are good for you. Know that you deserve it.

14.

Foundations for Recovery – Emotional Regulation Techniques

The contradictory and abusive actions of a narcissist can quite frankly leave you feeling like you are going mad. Parting ways with a narcissist is also painful and challenging. Narcissistic abuse is traumatising. It is stressful, anxiety-provoking, distressing and overwhelming at times. Another fundamental in recovery is finding ways in which you can help yourself manage difficult or overwhelming emotions. It can feel like being on an emotional roller coaster and so now it is important to find ways in which you can ease any overwhelm, to self-soothe, process and manage feelings – of which there will likely be a whole range. Below are some techniques to try to help with this:

MINDFULNESS

Mindfulness is the practice of psychological awareness. Practising mindfulness basically means to focus your awareness, to the present moment, in a curious, neutral and non-judgemental way (Kabat-Zinn, 2013). It is a simple practice that in time can have a powerful and positive impact on your thinking, feelings and behaviour. Studies have shown that the practice of mindfulness and mindfulness-based therapy can help with addictions (Chiesa & Serretti, 2013), ease depression and anxiety (Hofmann, Sawyer, Witt & Oh, 2010), increase tolerance and the ability to deal with distressing situations as well as to increase a sense of relaxation (Baer, 2003). It helps to manage and ease overwhelming emotions. Mindfulness practice also helps us to identify our thinking more clearly – it creates some distance to our experience. Practising mindfulness and developing mindful awareness will also be helpful for other aspects of recovery covered in later chapters.

So mindfulness is the practice of trying to focus the mind. One mindfulness meditation technique to get started with is called 'Mindfulness of Breath'.

Step by step guide to mindfulness of breath meditation:

1. Find a quiet place and time where you won't be interrupted.
2. Set a timer for the meditation. 5-10 minutes is a good time to start with and increase with practice, aiming for 20-30 minutes.
3. Settle in a seated position that is comfortable for you. Could be on a cushion, on the floor, on a chair or even lying down.
4. To begin with, take a few long, slow and deep breaths, relaxing the mind and any physical tensions.
5. Gently turn your attention to your breath. Mentally follow and track the inhalations and the exhalations.
6. Follow the natural flow of your breath. No need to try to force or control it.
7. At the end of every exhalation simply count, 1.
8. Continue following the breath and counting at the end of every exhalation. Inhale, exhale, 1... inhale, exhale, 2... inhale, exhale, 3... and so on.
9. Focus your attention on the breath and counting at the end of every exhalation. See if you can get to 10. If you get to 10

counts, simply start again at 1 and continue again. (If you get to 10 without losing your focus you are doing well!).

10. You may well notice thoughts pop into your mind or other distractions momentarily take you off track. Simply recognise that and gently return your focus and attention back to counting your breath. You may even like to label whatever the distraction was that you noticed; for example *'there's the thought that tells me I should be doing something else'*, or *'I noticed the thought 'I should be better at this by now''*.

The practice of mindfulness requires a level of awareness and alertness. Try not to allow yourself to just zone out – that is not the aim. As you try to focus on your breath, and count each exhalation, you may also notice anything else that comes up for you or that tries to pull your attention. Perhaps random thoughts come into your mind or you notice any physical sensations. Whatever it is, the practice of mindfulness simply means to notice it, label it and continue to refocus on the object of your mindfulness practice – in this case the breath. It is the noticing, the observing in a non-judgemental way of all that the mind throws up for you in distraction that is the real practice. It's the being vigilant to it, the noticing it, without getting pulled along any of the distractions or stories our minds will want to entice us with. It's the gentle unhooking from mental threads, again, not in a scorning, harsh or critical way, but in a gentle, curious manner, perhaps even bringing a sense of humour to it… *"ah, there's my mental 'to-do' list again"*… Just notice, don't judge. With mindfulness of breath, it's about constantly learning to notice when the mind has wandered (and it will because that's what minds do!). But learning to be vigilant to that, notice when that happens and when it does, gently unhook yourself and your attention from it and gently return it to the object of observation, the breath. If you find you have been distracted and have lost count, no bother, it will happen! Just gentle return your focus and start again at one. That is the practice.

For some people, it may seem too easy, too difficult or feel pointless. I hear many people say they have tried mindfulness meditation a few times, didn't like it, didn't understand it, didn't get any benefits from it and stopped – all very understandable. However, I would really encourage you to try and dedicate some time to this practice, on a daily basis for at least 2 weeks and then see if you notice any difference. Whilst counting your breath or practicing other mindfulness techniques may seem somewhat abstract, the power in this practice starts to come with time and really gets interesting and powerful when mindfulness starts to apply to your thoughts and feelings. The moment you become mindfully aware of something, is the moment you create some distance to it. That can be extremely powerful when it comes to unhelpful thoughts, inaccurate beliefs or overwhelming feelings. It's an important fundamental in your recovery and wellbeing. In time, it can also help with developing self-compassion. These are all important fundamentals in recovery from narcissistic abuse. Mindfulness meditation can bring about a sense of peace. That is likely a welcome respite. For now, adding a solid mindfulness practice into your daily routine will help support a useful foundation.

R.A.I.N

The acronym R.A.I.N is a 4-step mindfulness practice coined in recent years by insight meditation teacher Michele McDonald. It is a helpful systematic practice to help ease difficult or overwhelming emotions or feelings.

R – The 'R' stands for **RECOGNISE**. Recognise what it is you are feeling. It may be an emotion or a physical sensation – perhaps both. Name it. '*Anger*', '*Heat*'. Label whatever it is.

A – **ACCEPT** that this is what you are noticing right now. **ALLOW** your experience to be. *'OK, there is anxiety'*.

I – The next step is then to **INVESTIGATE**. What does this feeling, feel like? What's it like to feel that? What do I notice in my body? Is there anything else that goes with that?

N – **NON-ATTACHMENT** or **NON-IDENTIFYING** means creating some distance by observing our experience and not identifying it as 'me'. When you observe, you create distance. This can ease the intensity and attachment to your emotional experience.

GROUNDING TECHNIQUES

Grounding techniques helps ease overwhelming emotions or distress and can also support more realistic thinking. It brings a more objective and balanced perspective. Often when hit with the sudden switching, mood change, gas-lighting or rage of a narcissist, as well as our own anxiety, panic, guilt, shame or trauma, we can be completely thrown off balance. Many actions of the narcissist are designed to destabilise others, as that is how power is gained and maintained. Being thrown off track, feeling unsettled, bamboozled and confused all puts us in a vulnerable position of susceptibility for further self-doubt and abuse. When old traumatic memories are touched on, this can also leave us feeling triggered, 'floaty', shaky, anxious, panicky, racing mind, spaced out, frozen, paralysed, detached or dissociated. It is important to learn ways to ground and centre yourself in order to reduce the level of vulnerability to narcissistic abuse and trauma reaction as well as to help manage any overwhelm of emotions and reactions. Finding ways to feel more centred and grounded offers a sense of self-protection, it helps you to feel stronger in yourself and importantly supports the management of healthy boundaries and communication with narcissists. When we feel grounded and centred we are much less likely to be pulled and pushed around by any of the narcissists attempts to derail or destabilise us. When we are grounded we are able to feel much more self-assured. It helps us to see narcissistic abuse with more clarity.

We can ground and centre ourselves in a number of different ways. I would suggest trying a number of different techniques and see which work best for you.

ANCHORING IN THE BREATH

One technique is to anchor your attention to your breath. Often when we start to feel triggered or are confronted with narcissistic abuse, in the moment our breath instantly quickens and becomes shallow. This in itself can contribute to feeling more panicked and wobbly as the change in breath sends an immediate message to the brain that suggests there is a threat or an imminent danger of some kind. The brain then triggers messages to the nervous system that puts us in alert or 'fight or flight' mode. This can all happen within a split second, it is automatic. We can consciously slow down and deepen our breathing to help calm this inner alarm system and to allow a sense of grounding and 'anchoring' to arise. It may even help to visualise lowering down a heavy anchor in the breath and the body – imagining a downward pull through the breath, body and feet to feel more sturdy. Slow, deep, rhythmic breathing can help manage feelings of panic and help us maintain more equilibrium. Try slow breathing and continue for at least 5 minutes in order to calm the nervous system.

COUNTING THE BREATH

Slow, even breathing can also help us to feel more stable and grounded. Try inhaling and exhaling for the same count. Inhale for 1-2-3-4, pause for 1-2-3-4, exhale, 1-2-3-4, pause 1-2-3-4, inhale and continue. Slow and steady breathing helps support a steady and balanced mind.

USING THE SENSES

Another way to ground or centre yourself is to use your senses. Look around. Notice all that you see. Name all the items or things you see in your mind or out loud.

Reach and touch objects around you. Notice what it feels like to touch. Is it cold, warm, heavy, light, soft, hard, smooth, textured?

What can you smell? Notice any scents in or around where you are right now. You can focus on your own perfume or aftershave. Perhaps carry a welcoming scent or calming aromatherapy balm to use at stressful times. Focus your attentions on the smell.

Listen to the sounds inside and outside of where you are. Differentiate between the two. What can you hear that is nearest to you? Furthest away? What are those sounds?

Taste. Eat something. Eat mindfully. Focus on what it feels like, the texture, what it tastes like.

Again, this is where a solid mindfulness practice can help so that you are well practised in observing in a non-judgemental way. It can be a huge help in calming emotions and slowing racing minds and thoughts. It can help moments to feel more manageable. The more you practise this at quieter regular times, the more you will find you will more easily and more automatically apply these helpful techniques at more distressing or challenging times.

GROUNDING THROUGH THE FEET

Plant your feet on the ground about hip width apart. Sense your feet grounding into the earth or floor where you are standing. Gently shift your weight on both feet. Shift your weight slightly forwards to your toes and then back towards your heels, as well as side to side. Notice how that feels. Try to notice exactly where you experience the contact in your feet with the ground. Find a central balance point that feels good for you and focus your energy into sensing down into your legs, calves, ankles and feet and down into the ground. Enjoy the stabilising and strengthening sense that offers.

You might also like to imagine your feet growing strong and firm roots that spread down into the ground or floor beneath you. Like a tree with strong roots, visualise and imagine how much firmer the rest of you becomes, with those deep roots planted into the ground. A tree with firm roots is strong, sturdy and steady and much less likely to be blown by the wind (or the reactions and actions of a narcissist).

It might be good to actively move your feet. This is often the case if we feel a strong sense of 'fight or flight', an energy or urge to run, kick or move our legs and feet. Try walking on the spot. Lifting both feet, left and right. Noticing what that movement and energy feels like.

Or if you prefer something a little stronger, try stomping up and down on the ground. Or running on the spot. Play around with how strongly you stomp your feet, just noticing what that is like for you. Kicking your feet out is another option. Sense into whatever it is you feel your legs need, no matter how random that might seem.

Gently rubbing or massaging your feet can also be grounding, calming and soothing.

Mindfulness, breath work and grounding techniques can help manage times of overwhelm and they can also be useful to draw on when it comes to stating and holding boundaries or communicating with a narcissist (covered in later chapters). Play around and find what works best for you. Try to practice a little every day. The more you practice different techniques the easier they will be to use when you really need them.

15.

How to change how you feel by changing what you think

How we feel is influenced by what we are thinking. The kinds of thoughts that go through our minds have a direct impact on our feelings and mood. We can change the way we feel by changing our thinking. Our thoughts are very often subjective. Therefore our thoughts are changeable, they can be modified. We can learn to help ourselves feel better by first of all learning to recognise the sorts of unhelpful or inaccurate thoughts we have, and then by challenging and changing them. Recognising your thoughts is the first step and this can be supported by a mindfulness practice. Mindfulness helps us notice this more readily.

Imagine following a break-up you have thoughts along the lines of *"It's my fault"*, *"I'm never going to meet anybody again"*, *"Nobody will want me"*, *"I'm unattractive"*. It would not be a surprise that by having these sorts of thoughts that you will more than likely feel pretty low, hopeless or depressed. These thoughts are distorted though. Thoughts aren't facts. How might other people view the situation? How would a good friend see it? What would somebody that truly cared about you say? Perhaps something more along the lines of *"you are better off without him – he was horrible!"*, *"you are beautiful"*, *"you are a catch"*, *"you have the opportunity to meet other people now"*, or for yourself;

"I can enjoy spending more time with friends", *"I actually want some time on my own"*, *"I deserve better"*... How might you feel if you had more of those kinds of thoughts? Better?

The notion of changing your thoughts to help change how you feel comes from CBT. Cognitive Behavioural Therapy or CBT is a talking therapy used to help with a number of issues such as anxiety, depression, self esteem, OCD and eating disorders. The model can be helpful for some of the allied complaints related to narcissistic abuse, for example anxiety or self esteem. The model helps you to manage issues by understanding the link between your thoughts, your feelings and your actions. What we think affects how we feel and what we feel then influences what we do. The link between thoughts, feelings and behaviours goes around and around all day for us in various ways, however we usually barely notice. When we are troubled by negative or unhelpful thoughts, or difficult feelings however, it can then be helpful to pay more attention to what is happening in this psychological loop. By starting to notice the thoughts that go through your mind, in time you can work to slow down, break down, challenge and change any unhelpful or negative thought patterns – thus helping yourself to feel better and make wiser behavioural choices for yourself.

Recognising, challenging or changing any negative or unhelpful thoughts, to more positive, accurate or helpful ones can have an immediate and direct impact on how you feel. Thought challenging techniques can help you to do that. In this way, problems are broken down into five main areas:

* situation
* thoughts
* feelings / emotions
* physical sensations
* behaviour / actions

To give you an example, your relationship has ended (situation) and you think that it is your fault, that you've failed and that you will never meet anybody again (thoughts). These kinds of thoughts or beliefs will likely leave you or anybody else for that matter feeling pretty hopeless, guilty, lonely and depressed (feelings). These feelings often go alongside feeling fatigued, empty or heavy (physical feelings). As a result you may then isolate yourself, staying in alone at home, or perhaps drinking or eating excessively because of the way you are feeling (behaviour / actions). By isolating, drinking or eating excessively you will in turn only likely further fuel the negative cycle. Such behaviours may then lead to further unhelpful thoughts or beliefs about yourself and so the downward spiral continues. But what if you stop? What if you put the brakes on and learn to first of all identify any unhelpful thinking. Try to notice what the actual thoughts or beliefs are that go through your mind and try to pause at that point. Then you can get into the habit of questioning the validity of those thoughts. Once you recognise your unhelpful or perhaps inaccurate thoughts, then question:

> *Is this really true? Is this absolutely true all of the time? Is this subjective? What would I think if I was to be totally objective? If a friend was telling me he/she thought this what would I say to them? What might be a more objective, rational way of thinking about this?*

Remember **thoughts are not facts.** Thoughts can be challenged and changed. You can learn to challenge and change your own unhelpful thoughts to something that is perhaps arguably more realistic and certainly more helpful.

Lets imagine you then change the thoughts to something more along the lines of: *"It wasn't my fault the relationship broke down – it takes two", "It wasn't right or a healthy situation anyway", "I'm better off without that person in my life", "I'll find somebody new one day, but for now I can enjoy spending time with my friends and doing what I like"*... (thoughts) How do you imagine you may feel if you had more of these kinds of thoughts? You may likely feel better, less responsible or guilty, more hopeful or more connected (feelings). In turn you may also feel more positive and energised (physical feelings). As a result you may feel more motivated to see friends or go out to enjoy more of the things you like to do. To eat well and take good care of yourself (behaviours / actions).

Recognising, challenging and changing your thoughts is a simple yet powerful tool to help manage your feelings and actively work to help yourself feel better and to help make healthier decisions. To recap the steps are:

1. Recognise any particular unhelpful or inaccurate thoughts.
2. Notice how they may be influencing how you feel.
3. Ask yourself how helpful, positive or objective the thoughts are.
4. Think about what might be a more objective or helpful way of thinking about the situation or yourself. What would you say to a really good friend if you knew they were thinking or feeling this way?
5. What is a more balanced, helpful or realistic way of thinking about this?
6. How does the more helpful way of thinking leave you feeling?

You may find it helpful to journal your thoughts and findings. It can take a bit of practice and time with working on this but it is a helpful way of addressing any cognitive distortions that are negatively affecting how you feel or what you do. Sometimes our thoughts are so habitual it can be difficult to notice what they are at first. Do keep with it. Just like smoking, if you have smoked for ten or twenty years it is an engrained habit. Certain automatic thinking is a habit too. But just like smoking, with some effort and perseverance, it is a habit that can be broken. Our thinking habits can be changed. They can be changed to something more positive, helpful and arguably more accurate.

This tool is not a cure all, however it can be a helpful practical psychological technique to help with anxiety, depression, self esteem and other allied issues often associated with narcissistic abuse. It can be particularly useful to help to address any inaccurate or untrue thoughts or beliefs we may have about ourselves or our relationship. You may find it helpful to learn more via reading specific books or study guides. Working with a qualified CBT Therapist will help you to get to grips with the theory and techniques so that you can then apply on your own to a wide range of issues.

Reflection point:

* What reoccurring unhelpful thoughts or beliefs do you notice you have about yourself?
* What impact does this have on your self esteem?
* What impact does this have on your relationships?
* What would be a more helpful way of thinking?
* What would you say to a good friend or somebody else that you cared about if they were having similar negative or unhelpful thoughts about themselves or their situation? What would you suggest instead? How would you reassure or comfort them? What is it like to offer the same supportive words to yourself?
* Is there anything else you notice about the link between your thoughts, feelings and actions?

EXERCISE: MINDFULNESS OF THOUGHTS

As with the mindfulness of breathing exercise, begin by putting aside some time for yourself where you won't be interrupted.

Put a timer on for 5-15 minutes and find a comfortable seating place.

Take a few deep breaths to help calm your mind and body. Gently bring your attention to your breath.

Try to focus your conscious attention to your breath, following the inhalation and exhalation.

No need to force anything to happen or not happen.

The mind will naturally wander, because that is what it does. The aim here is to simply notice that happening.

No need to force or change anything. Just notice.

Focusing your attention gently on the breath, following the inhalation and exhalation, try to notice as and when any thoughts arise.

We don't need to make anything happen. Allow the thoughts to come and go… as they will…

Allow yourself to notice any thoughts that come into your head as you are focusing on the breath.

Notice any automatic thoughts for what they are… thoughts. They aren't necessarily facts.

We don't need to get swept away with judging our thoughts, trying to decide if we like them or not, if they are the sorts of thoughts that we want or don't want. Just notice…

It can be helpful to preface with "I am noticing the thought…" and try to capture whatever the thought is, no matter how random, strange or difficult it may be.

You may notice a flurry of thoughts, or it may be the odd thought you notice.

Again, there is no need to try and make anything happen or not happen. We are watching that quite naturally our minds will have all sorts of thoughts. We don't need to give them any

*more power than that. By observing them, we can see them just
for what they are.*

*Notice what it is like as you notice and identify any
thoughts? You may notice they are replaced with other
thoughts. You may notice that thoughts come and go.*

*Any time you notice your mind has wandered off along a
stream of thoughts, then gently just notice that and bring your
attention back to the breath as an anchor for this meditation
practice.*

Practising 'mindfulness of thoughts' meditation is a powerful
exercise that in time can bring about a many number of benefits
for your own mental health and the relationship you have within
yourself. The relationship you have with yourself has a knock-
on effect to relationships with others. If and when you notice
any thoughts that suggest *"It's my fault"*, *"I didn't do it right"*,
"he's going to…", instead of instantly believing that as fact and
reacting to that, simply recognise it for what it is. *"ahh… theres
a thought that says 'it's my fault'… that doesn't necessarily mean
it is the case! In fact, I don't believe it is my fault… I tried my
best"*. From there you can build on adjusting your thoughts and
thinking habits to perhaps thoughts and beliefs that are more
helpful and quite likely more accurate.

The more you practice mindfulness the more you will
experience the benefits from it. Regularity is key, so even if you
manage just 10-15 minutes a day, if you can do this every day, it
will be helpful and impactful in a relatively short period of time.

For further support and instruction you might also like to
consider joining a local mindfulness or meditation group or
course. Finding a teacher or instructor can be really helpful
to ensure you are on the right tracks and to be able to ask any
questions you might have about your practice.

ADDRESSING DISTORTED
UNDERLYING BELIEFS

By practising mindfulness of thoughts exercises and trying to notice your automatic, unhelpful thoughts more and more, you may find that you have a few 'favourites'. These are the reoccurring ones we often have in various forms. We all have them. If they are not helpful or not serving you well though you may want to address them. Our underlying beliefs about ourselves, others or the world we live in acts as a bias or filter in which we interpret our experience. This core belief shapes and influences the sort of thoughts we tend to have. For example, if we notice we have thoughts along the lines of; *"I will never meet anyone again"*, *"People won't find me attractive or interesting"* or *"I don't deserve..."*, these thoughts may well be related to an underlying belief that *"I'm unlovable"* or *"I'm not worthy"*. Inaccurate thoughts arise from inaccurate beliefs. If you find that your habitual thoughts are of a particular theme it can be helpful then to address the underlying assumption or belief that is feeding those thoughts.

Narcissistic abuse often triggers a common core belief of *"I'm not good enough"*. In fact, feeling or believing *"I'm not enough"* or *"good enough"* in relation to someone is in itself a possible sign of being in relationship with a narcissist. That's because nothing and no-one is ever, and will never be good enough for a narcissist. This in a way reflects their own deep self-loathing and shame yet is projected out onto others via the judgemental and critical things they say and do and the messages they convey. Partners and children of narcissists often struggle chronically with self-esteem and this comes from an underlying sense of not being good enough, not doing enough, not being smart enough, slim enough, pretty enough, popular enough, confident enough, enough. A core belief of *not being good enough / enough* will fuel associated thoughts and thinking habits that go with that.

This may include thoughts that tell us we are not OK the way we are, so therefore we need to be slimmer, more attractive, work harder or achieve more. It relates to thoughts that are self-critical and judgemental. We may also find we compare ourselves a lot to others and in comparison feel less than. A narcissist will in various ways contribute to maintaining the belief that we are not enough the way we are. In turn fuelling our attempts to try and somehow gain the approval or satisfaction from the narcissist. Whether we are aware of it at the time or not, slowly but surely this underlying undermining will negatively affect a persons confidence and self-esteem. Trying to be enough for a narcissist is maddening and futile. Nothing and nobody is good enough for a narcissist. The most important thing you can do for your sanity is to recognise this and give up the fight. Recognise the futility of trying to appease a narcissist and instead focus on working on your own self-esteem, your core beliefs and the relationship you have with yourself. You are enough the way you are. For many of us though, especially if we are fresh from narcissistic abuse, this may not feel so easy to believe. You can work on building your inner beliefs though, to something more accurate, helpful and loving for you.

PRACTICAL EXERCISE FOR MODIFYING UNHELPFUL UNDERLYING BELIEFS:

A helpful practical exercise is to first of all recognise any core belief/s you have about yourself or others. This may become clear from noting any habitual negative thoughts you have as explained in the previous section. Common core beliefs in relation to narcissistic abuse include:

I'm not good enough
I'm unlovable

There's something wrong with me
It's my fault
I'm responsible
I'm unsafe

Get your journal and at the top of the page write down your unhelpful or negative underlying belief. eg. *"I'm not good enough"*. Then ask yourself *'What experiences do I have that show this belief is not always or necessarily true?'*. Write down as many as you can think of no matter how small they may be. These examples show that this belief is not always true all of the time. Then on a new page write your new positive self-belief. "I <u>am</u> good enough". From here list as many examples as you can from times when you have been good enough, when you have felt good and are enough. Examples from the day may include: *"I talked to my friend who is having a bad time – I'm a good friend"*, *"I did enough work"*, *"I'm a good enough cook"*, *"I was friendly to the staff in the coffee shop today – I'm a nice person"*, *"My hair looks good today"*… whatever it may be. Continue to add examples for the new positive belief every single day. Even if it's just a few from each day. Keep adding to it. Doesn't matter how big or small the examples may be. The main thing is to keep adding to it. Keep supporting your new belief with any kind of evidence at all until your perspective has become more balanced, positive and helpful. This is especially important in recovery from narcissistic abuse because during any form of emotional abuse the abuser sets to undermine how we feel about ourselves – to damage our self-esteem or self-belief. In time our perspective gets very skewed. It may be difficult to address this now, but you can get there. Build on new, more positive and more accurate beliefs, one step at a time. Bit by bit, make a point of acknowledging your attributes on a daily basis and in time you will build your self-esteem and improve the deep relationship you have with yourself.

"When things finally came to an end with Tim I felt like I'd just come out of a storm. I was traumatised and in a state of shock. The lies, betrayal and abuse had gotten so bad – I don't think I realised the full extent until he suddenly ended things again. I knew this time was the last time though – things had gotten so desperately crazy. During the relationship Tim would criticise me and make strange comments about most things I did. He would criticise my cooking and tease that I wasn't good at my job. It would be part in jest but it did really get to me. I used to like to run and he would even say that I didn't run correctly, that I looked silly. At the time, I don't think I really registered the things he would say. However, when I was left at the end of the relationship all his comments would play around in my mind. I spent weeks beating myself up for not having done all these things correctly. Convinced that he had left me because I couldn't do things right. I started to recognise my self-talk – it was so harsh and critical. I was shocked at how relentless it was. It was as if my brain had absorbed all his nasty comments over the years and was now replaying them. No wonder I was feeling so desperately depressed and frustrated. I could do nothing but cry in bed for weeks after the final break-up. A friend suggested I speak to somebody and they helped me to recognise the unhelpful thoughts I was having. All the self criticism was like a broken record going round and round my mind. I also recognised I did a lot of comparison. Imagining that if I was thinner, prettier or funnier then things would have been fine. But the truth is nothing I could do or be would have ever been good enough for him – and that's his issue. I realised how much all his comments had destroyed my self-esteem and reinforced this deep belief that I am not good enough and that nothing I do or could ever do would be good enough. I started to chip away at this destructive belief that he had fed in me. Slowly but surely, bit by bit, I started to notice and write down times when I was OK and good enough. I am fit enough,

I am more than intelligent enough, I am a good person. I'm a good friend. I am funny. By writing examples down every day I felt much better in just a few weeks. Like my vision and judgement had been destroyed. It was actually like getting a new pair of glasses with the right lens in! I could see more clearly. I am OK and I am good enough, just the way I am. The constant criticisms reflect his issues and his insecurities and he is welcome to keep them!"

Good self-esteem and self-belief relates to our ability to hold healthy and firm boundaries. Working on your self-esteem via these techniques can aid the development of healthier boundaries and as you work on your boundaries they in turn also help you to feel good about yourself.

Reflection point:

* What underlying beliefs do I recognise?
* What are the core beliefs that might fuel my fears or unhelpful thinking?
* What is a more positive belief I might have about myself?
* What evidence can I find to support my new, more positive (and arguably) more accurate belief?

For further help or guidance with this please see the References & Further Reading section at the end of this book or find a CBT Therapist to work directly with.

16.

Foundation for Recovery – Boundaries

Healthy boundaries are essential to healthy relationships. Learning about and developing healthy personal boundaries is an absolutely vital fundamental in the managing of, and recovery from narcissistic and other dysfunctional or abusive relationships. Firm yet flexible boundaries are the very thing that protects us from these kinds of destructive dynamics. With healthy boundaries we have a more balanced perspective and are less concerned or troubled by what the other person is doing or not doing.

We all communicate our boundaries in a number of different ways. Via verbal communication, what we say and how we say it and we also communicate energetically via our body language. Boundaries are both a clear and invisible communication. It is something that we communicate both in terms of what we put out as well as what we receive and pick up on in other people. I mentioned before in an earlier chapter about how narcissists and echoists seemingly have a magnetic pull to one another. Almost as if we can seek the other out in a crowd. We are drawn to and attract a 'match'. In one sense it is the dysfunctional fit of boundary issues that support the magnetic draw to one another. This stops when one side changes. Narcissists have no respect for boundaries and will naturally and instinctively be drawn to people who either have none, or have flimsy, easily pushed over and malleable boundaries. Narcissists have more chance of getting what they want with somebody they can manipulate. Similarly, those with weak boundaries are often on some level seeking out somebody with firm, direct and assertive wants, and needs and capability of decision making. Sometimes they seek a partner so they can retreat and step back within the relationship.

Personal boundaries then are essentially an invisible shield of protection that serve to keep the owner of those boundaries safe, as well as providing containment for ourselves and others. When we respect other peoples boundaries we are helping them to feel safe. Boundaries define an individuals limits, both for themselves as well as for anybody else they may be in any kind of relationship with. Boundaries help both parties to know where they stand. They are protective and containing for all. Our boundaries establish – to both ourselves and to others – what we deem appropriate and acceptable in terms of physical or emotional closeness, sexual contact, mental or psychological intimacy, communication, as well as what we regard 'OK' or 'not OK' in behaviours and actions – both our own and others. Boundaries portray our sense of likes and dislikes and preferences to others. They also reflect our values, self-esteem and self-worth to others. Healthy boundaries are essential in any kind of relationship, whether it be romantic, family, professional or friendships.

Working on your own boundaries is important to help you manage any relationship but especially any relationship you have with a narcissist. Firm, healthy boundaries are also key to developing the strength to leave or end an unhealthy or abusive relationship with a narcissist or bully. A strong sense of your own boundaries goes hand in hand with a strong sense of your values, self-esteem and self-worth. So knowing your values (ie. what's important to you and how you want to live), knowing your self-worth and having good enough self-regard and firm grasp and understanding of boundaries are protective factors that ensure you are a lot less likely to tolerate any abusive behaviour from anybody. It also makes you less attractive to narcissists and bullies in the first place. With a strong sense of your values, self-esteem, self-worth and firm boundaries you are much more easily able to say *"no"* and to make it clear to others that their abusive, manipulative, unpleasant behaviours or comments are unacceptable. This comes with knowing wholeheartedly that you do not want it or need it because you know that you deserve better. You set your rules.

Boundaries serve to keep people from coming into our space and abusing us; sexually, physically, psychologically and emotionally, as well as to keep us from doing the same to other people. They also support a shared and mutual sense of a separation. It distinguishes who we are and who we are not within a dynamic – in relation to ourselves and other people. Boundary systems serve two parts – internal and external. Without boundaries there are no clear limits for either party, it is impossible for either side to know where they stand. That leads to relationship chaos. Narcissists do not have healthy boundaries and a narcissist will rarely respect anybody else's. They will however, push and manipulate other peoples boundaries in order to try to get what *they* want – regardless of the harm or discomfort it causes anyone. Because remember, narcissists are only concerned with what they want. It is all about them all of the time – even if they may appear caring, comforting, concerned or respectful.

WHERE DO BOUNDARIES COME FROM?

We first tend to develop our sense of personal boundaries during our childhood and this is usually shaped by what is taught and modelled to us by our parents and family. Boundaries come from what we learn about our minds, bodies and our personal space. Early life experiences, early relationships, our family and household dynamics all influence our understanding and practice of boundary systems both in terms of our own as well as how we might respond to or respect other peoples. In an ideal childhood our emerging development of personal boundary is encouraged and supported so that we develop a firm sense of this within the family unit and subsequently in other relationships. This is typically learnt through having our space and belongings, our bodies and minds, our thoughts and feelings all acknowledged and respected as well as being shown how to respect other peoples. Through this we learn the separation between ourselves and others. We learn that some things are ours and that we have a choice as to whether we want to share them or not. We learn it is OK to say 'no'. We ideally learn that we can have our own personal space, psychologically and physically and that others should and do respect that. This includes our belongings, our bedrooms, our bodies. For example, we can use the bathroom without anybody bursting through the door or that our childhood bedroom is a space that is ours and is respected. Many clients I work with who have ended up in narcissistically abusive relationships are often surprised about how this can link back to seemingly very simple yet formative experiences of boundary issues growing up. Parents who constantly barge into a childs bedroom or space without knocking are demonstrating a violation of a boundary. A child is usually unable to do anything about that as being a child we are restricted with conforming to doing as we are told by the adults around us. So potentially this is how we learn that it's OK for people to invade their space – *"it's what they do"*. Another fairly common experience is being mocked, ridiculed or bullied as a child when we have tried to say 'no' or express our preferences or wishes. Common boundary issues in families also include adults exposing or discussing adult matters with children or adolescents. Adults/parents should contain adult-stuff whilst allowing children to enjoy a safe and carefree as possible childhood. This containment is a healthy parent/child boundary. It is common that as children we were exposed to adult difficulties that were confusing for us to really make sense of. Perhaps as children we were forced to keep quiet, to be good, to comply, to not resist or upset others – we had little choice. However, as adults now we do.

Childhoods are rarely perfect. If our parents or family members did not understand or learn healthy boundaries themselves, then it is highly unlikely that they would be able to model or teach this to anybody else. Of course, different generations and cultures reflect different views and ideals about families and boundaries too. Whilst a lack of boundaries may be normalised in some family systems, it invariably creates chaos and dysfunction. It also impacts on mental and emotional health. Healthy boundaries are needed in order to enjoy fulfilling interdependent relationships. Any past experiences of a violation to our personal boundaries of any kind can create difficulties in maintaining firm healthy boundaries. For many of us, healthy boundaries are something we actively seek to learn or refine as adults.

UNDERSTANDING BOUNDARIES

One way to begin to understand boundaries is to imagine a fence in the garden that surrounds a house you inhabit. The fence marks your land, it outlines your space. The fence clearly defines the boundary space for you and others to see. Much like a nice home, the fence is approachable. It is of a height that allows you to see over it and for others to see over from the other side. Both sides can interact and communicate with the other. Lets imagine there is also a gate, so there is an option for movement. There is an opening for yourself and other people to go in and out. This garden fence analogy is a way of demonstrating what a healthy middle-ground boundary looks like. The boundary is clear for everybody, there is room to move, to see over it and to offer access, to open or close it. There is room for negotiation or flexibility if both parties wish to negotiate it. It is a healthy medium and healthy balance point.

In contrast, extreme boundary polarities include having absolutely no fence at all. With no fence nobody knows where the boundary edge is, or even if there is any. I'm sure you can imagine what kind of chaos that would cause between neighbours or passers by. I once lived in a lovely house that had no fence, there was no clear boundary edge. There were often people walking up to the windows and children playing in the garden, driveway and right up by the front door! It always used to surprise me that people would encroach so closely to my windows, seemingly blissfully unaware that it was my space. But, without a clear marked boundary, how was anybody to know? It's much the same with your own personal boundaries. With no boundary or parameters it is basically an invite for anybody and everybody to walk over the garden to play and mess around in. Children, adults, the nearby dogs and cats could use the space to mess. The unboundaried space could even be used as a car park if somebody even wanted to! With no boundary there are no clear or defined limits. Nobody knows where they stand. There are no parameters, guidelines or rules. If we do not have clear boundaries of our own, we are essentially inviting people to walk all over us and do or take as they want. More often than not then we are the ones then left feeling resentful, upset or suffering.

At the opposite end of the spectrum is having overly strong, rigid boundaries. This is the equivalent of having incredibly tall, hard, rigid brick walls all the way around the property. Nobody can see over or get in or out. With this comes a very strong and powerful message for others to stay well away. There is no room whatsoever for movement or negotiation. No flexibility.

This is equally unhealthy as having no boundary. Walls and inflexible boundaries relate to avoidance, control and rigidity in relationships. As with anything, extremes of any kind are rarely healthy. Instead you can find balance somewhere in between the extremes... a healthy middle ground.

Below are essentially the three basic types of boundaries that are relevant to narcissistic abuse and more importantly, your recovery process.

Non-existent or Flimsy: This reflects having no or little sense of boundary or of what is OK or not OK for you. With this type of boundary there is a real and dangerous risk of blurring and merging with other people. This includes becoming enmeshed or letting people take the lead, or more specifically and more worryingly, manipulate and take advantage. Non-existent or flimsy boundaries are seen in people who have difficulty identifying and expressing their needs, wants or likes to others or who have issues for whatever reason with saying '*no*'. They tend to like what other people are into without having much clear sense of their own likes, needs or individual identity. Those with weak, flimsy boundaries may also relate to traits and characteristics of codependency. Such little sense of personal boundaries are often seen in people from dysfunctional families, perhaps where there are mental health issues or problems with alcoholism, addictions or abuse. Non-existent or flimsy boundaries also relate to those with experience of having their boundaries violated or have childhoods where they were never shown how to have healthy boundaries, for example, never having their personal space or emotional experience acknowledged or respected. Those with no or poor boundaries are susceptible to manipulation and abuse. Sometimes people with non-existent or poor boundaries find they swing from one extreme to the other. Demonstrating zero boundary in some situations whilst then being completely rigid and inflexible in others.

Rigid and Extreme: Rigid and extreme boundaries are pretty much the complete opposite to non-existent or flimsy boundaries and many people mistakingly view this as positive. Often I have seen people who take up an extreme opposite position of radical and rigid rules and restrictions in the false understanding that this demonstrates a healthy boundary. It is not. It is more like having huge and tall brick walls as boundaries. Nobody or anything can move, get in or out. Healthy boundaries are balanced. Many people with extreme rigid boundaries are actually very fearful or controlling of others. The rigid or extreme 'boundaries' (or walls) serve to keep people away and at a distance. It is equally difficult to enjoy real emotional intimacy and interpersonal closeness with extreme boundaries, as it is to have none.

Healthy – Firm yet Flexible: A healthy sense of personal boundary reflects a balance point that lies in between flimsy and rigid boundaries. It is the nice, friendly, approachable garden fence, low enough to see over, but high enough to offer some safety and security. There is also a gate or opening and therefore some room for movement and negotiation. This type of boundary describes a sense of knowing what is yours and what is not, what is your responsibility and what is not, knowing who you are, knowing what you want and need, being able to attend to your own wants and needs responsibly as well as being able to communicate those things effectively with others. It is also a space where you feel comfortable saying no and asserting yourself with other people – in a balanced, considerate and neutral way. Healthy boundaries allow for some degree of flexibility given the individual relationship, dynamic or situation. Healthy flexibility in boundaries means being able to have some movement, without losing your sense of self or what is right for you.

With healthy boundaries come a clear sense of
what is yours and what is not; what is your
responsibility and importantly, what is not

Not only do healthy boundaries help to mark this out for yourself, it also helps to make this clear to others. This in turn encourages both parties to take responsibility for themselves. Whilst there is no guarantee that other people will take responsibility for themselves appropriately, your own healthy boundaries make it clear that it is their responsibility (and not yours) regardless.

Developing and establishing your own boundaries are key
to managing relationship dynamics with a narcissist

Healthy boundaries clearly communicate your sense of dignity, self-worth, values and self-esteem. Without boundaries you lay yourself wide open to hurt and abuse and run the risk of negatively affecting others in the same way. A narcissist has unhealthy boundaries and does not care about yours, or anybody elses. In fact, many people with antisocial, borderline or narcissistic personality traits will instinctively become hellbent on trying to pull and push boundaries whether consciously or otherwise. It is especially important, for your relationships and your own sanity, that yours are clear and firm.

An abusive narcissist is selfish and manipulative so you can be sure that they will try to push and bend your boundaries in whichever way they can in order to get what they want. Remember, they believe they are absolutely entitled to whatever they want, whenever they want it. This manipulation may be in the form of saying mean things to get you to back down, bullying tactics, lies, manipulation, gas-lighting, guilt-tripping and so on.

Tracy• was a client I had been seeing for about 6 months. She had a family background of non-existent and flimsy boundaries as well as specific experiences of repeated violation of her personal boundaries by both parents when she was young. This was in the sense of her personal physical and psychological space not being supported or respected. Effectively, she had grown up in a family where boundaries were not encouraged or modelled. In fact the message was effectively that to state any sense of self-assurance in this way showed that you were being 'selfish' and 'self-important'… Any attempt at naming what was not OK in the family was met with name calling and a scathing "Who do you think you are?", "You think you are so much better than us" – type response from her parents. Understandably, soon enough Tracy learnt to drop any attempt to state or even sense her limits and eventually lost her sense of boundaries and sense of her own wants or needs. She disconnected. This is quite common in childhood, where self-care and stating boundaries is met with criticism and judgement or where there is a message of martyrdom in being selfless, 'altruistic' or being more concerned with others needs than your own self-care. As an adult, Tracy repeatedly found herself in abusive relationships with male narcissist partners where she would report that she would feel OK in the beginning of a relationship, before then slowly but surely losing a sense of herself. She would take on her partners hobbies and interests and neglect her own self care needs or wants, often stopping seeing her friends. At work, she also had a bullyish female boss and felt unable to say no to extra work demands that were put on her on a regular basis. Any attempt at trying to state when things did not feel OK for her, she would experience a visceral block in her throat, as if the words were stuck and she had lost her voice.

During our therapy work together we focused on developing healthier boundaries. This started with understanding and *making sense of the kinds of messages she had learnt whilst growing up from her parents about boundaries and how boundaries were viewed in the family system. As an adult now, Tracy was able to recognise the importance and use of boundaries and was able to start to let go of the historic, inaccurate and damaging view her parents had of this. We then worked on developing her internal sense of boundary as well as a physical external sense of her 'space'. This often goes hand in hand with a developing sense of self-esteem and worth. Working on identifying her values, likes and dislikes in various areas of her life was also helpful. In time, Tracy was able to start to find her voice and communicate her personal boundaries, specifically stating what was OK and not OK for her in her work place and personal relationships. I encouraged her to start small and experiment, play around with sensing into what it feels like to say no or state her own preferences in day to day situations. This way you can learn in small steps. She had by now, developed a clearer understanding of what constitutes a healthy relationship. In response to her attempts to clarify her boundary in her romantic relationship, her narcissistic partner began to tease her about her 'new boundaries' and reiterated the same kind of response her parents had given her as a youngster. "Who do you think you are laying down the law!?", "You think you are so above everybody now, don't you, with all your therapy talk or boundaries this and boundaries that". This is so clearly a narcissists way of trying to manipulate and regain the power and control in the relationship – in the face of this changing, as it does when you learn to establish healthy boundaries for yourself. It was a particularly cruel attempt of his at knocking down her boundaries especially given that he was using the same lines he knew full well her parents had told her when she was younger. Fortunately, Tracy had by that point enough new understanding and strong enough self-esteem (and frankly had had enough of repeating bad relationship patterns) that she was able to see his response for what it was (ie. his). She held close and firm to her boundaries and her sense of what was OK and not OK for her. She had the strength to leave him shortly afterwards and she continued to rebuild her self-worth and self-esteem, breaking the pattern of dysfunctional and unhealthy relationships.*

Remember: the only people who will get upset about you setting boundaries are the ones who benefit from you having none

Boundaries are communicated in a number of ways both verbally and non-verbally. We can learn to clearly communicate our boundaries in a direct verbal manner, articulating them assertively to others. Boundaries are also communicated non-verbally, through our body language, energy and mannerisms. If you put 1000 people in one room, I am convinced a narcissist will somehow automatically sense the person or persons in attendance with flimsy or non-existent boundaries before any words are even exchanged – and they will make a straight beeline for each other. There is an invisible magnetic pull in this dynamic. But the good news is that it only takes one to change in order to alter this attraction. That person can be you. You can improve your personal boundary – internally and externally – and by doing so, improve your self-esteem and your relationships.

The firmer your boundaries are, the easier it is for others to pick up on this. The firmer your boundaries are, the more difficult it is for others to rattle, push over or weaken them. This is crucial for your wellbeing, sense of responsibility and your own sanity, as well as for the health of your relationships.

<u>You</u> are responsible for <u>your own</u> personal boundaries.
You are <u>not</u> responsible for anybody else's.

17.   Mastering Healthy Boundaries

HEALTHY RELATIONSHIPS RELY ON HEALTHY BOUNDARIES

Personal boundaries serve to contain and mark our individual space, to protect and contain both ourselves and others. It creates a kind of invisible shield around us that holds our sense of what feels OK for us. Boundaries help us communicate to others where our sense of personal space is, what is acceptable or not for us, what we want, need or prefer. Boundaries support accountability. Different types of personal boundaries include: physical, psychological, emotional and sexual.

A narcissist has little sense or regard for boundaries. Similarly, those of us drawn to narcissists (and are attractive *to* narcissists) will often not have as good boundaries as we might like to believe, or indeed, need. We may mistakingly consider ourselves as just *'easy going'* or *'selfless'* when we don't assert our wants, dislikes, needs or preferences. Or we may struggle to say *'no'* in the face of a volatile, threatening or angry narcissist. We may experience fear or guilt that interferes with our ability to hold healthy boundaries. Some of us may be confused about why we feel we hold fairly good, solid boundaries at work or with the children or friends, only for any sense of this to fall to the wayside as soon as Mr or Mrs Narcissist is on the scene. Many people I have worked with report that trying to hold firm boundaries with a narcissist is exhausting. It can certainly feel like that whilst you are learning and sensing into finding your way with this, but in time you will almost certainly find that having a clearer sense of boundaries is in fact very freeing. Healthy, firm boundaries make for easier relationships all round and is actually rather energy-preserving and energising in opposed to being draining.

SO WHAT DOES HAVING HEALTHY BOUNDARIES REALLY MEAN?

Healthy boundaries reflect a sense of who you are, what you like, what you don't like, what's acceptable to you and what is not. It also includes a sense of personal responsibility – knowing what it is your responsibility as well as what is not. This also includes recognising what is within your control and what is not. Partners of abusers tend to have poor, weak boundaries and this has to be addressed as part of recovery.

It is important to note though that healthy personal boundaries does not mean suddenly becoming icy cold, stern and rigid. Many times, it is all too easy to make the mistake of going from one extreme to the other when it comes to boundaries. Either having no boundaries, very loose, easily pushed and knocked down boundaries or the other extreme of having tall walls – the shutters comes down and we become closed and rigid – this is equally unhealthy. As with most things, a healthy place can be found in the middle balance point. Healthy boundaries are *firm yet flexible*. It may take going from one extreme to the other as you manage this relationship and in order to find your balance point in time.

One key issue related to boundaries that many people who have experienced narcissistic abuse get stuck at, is one of where your focus and attention is. Because of the trauma these kinds of relationships can bring, it is common, and to some extent quite understandable for partners and exes to become pre-occupied or fixated on all the ex/partner did or didn't or is currently doing. The things they said, or continue to say, didn't say, what they are doing now, where they are going, with who, how much weight they have lost/gained, what they are earning or spending their money on, what they are posting on social media, why?, etc. etc, etc.

> **Please note: Too much attention and focus on the narcissist and not enough on yourself is the problem in the first place!**

This must stop in order to recover, heal and move on.

GAME, SET, MATCH

In order to further illustrate healthy boundaries, at this stage I'd like you to imagine you are watching a game of tennis. Your seat is central, positioned along the mid-way point, with a perfect view of the whole court. On one side of the court is the narcissist, ready to serve. On the other side is you. The net in the middle represents the boundary.

In healthy relationships, the boundary between two people is usually fairly central – with room and flexibility for both people to move, shift and fluctuate, much like players do during a game of tennis. Sometimes one is nearer to the boundary, other times further away. This is usually according to, and in appropriate response to the individual and relationship dynamic, context and situation.

Healthy relationships are enjoyed when two people are able and willing to gently and largely stay on their own sides of the

Boundaries – where each person takes care of and responsibility for their own actions and needs

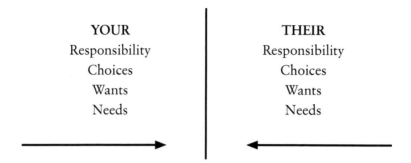

YOUR	THEIR
Responsibility	Responsibility
Choices	Choices
Wants	Wants
Needs	Needs

court. Each individual then takes care of their own responsibilities including knowing and communicating their own choices, their own wants, needs, likes and dislikes, as well as respecting all of that and the boundary in and of the other person. Healthy relationships are when two people are at least mostly willing and able to do this.

There is a healthy meet in the middle – with some room for flexibility and negotiation depending on whatever is happening at any given time. However, overall it is fairly even and balanced. Importantly, staying on your side of the court can help encourage the other person to stay on their side too – although this is not a guarantee. In other words having a healthy level of personal self-care and self-responsibility invites the other person to move forward to develop a more healthy and appropriate level of personal responsibility and to take care of their own self-care needs. If you attend to your own responsibilities, wants and needs, this allows others to do the same.

If you are busy doing too much for the other person, running over to their side of the court, taking on too much responsibility that is not even yours, then *you* are not leaving any space for them to play their part. You effectively block them from being able to manage themselves and their responsibilities, choices or needs. This is actually often what narcissists want – this is often what they will invite people to do. Narcissists can and will try to pull people into that position. Some of us are keen and ready to jump into that role; to rescue or fix or take responsibility for – and that is usually because it keeps us distracted and away from our own issues, our own anxieties or emotions. We have to recognise we play a part in that. You need to focus on what *you* are doing – and what you are doing, on your side of the court, in your half of the relationship, is *your* responsibility. It is up to you to do something about what you are doing. It is not for you to stray over to the other side of the court and over-concern yourself with what is happening there. The other side, the other half of the relationship is not within your control and it is not your responsibility. If you find yourself habitually or compulsively drawn over to the other side then it can be useful to use the 4-step process to help let it go and to bring your focus back to yourself. Then you are more able to work on whatever it is that is going on for you that propels you to focus so much on somebody else. Often it is about our own discomfort, anxiety or guilt that we need to work to let go of.

In order for a game of tennis to be enjoyed, it requires, and indeed the rules are, that each participant stays on their own side of the court. Both sides then equally engage in the play. In a relationship, each players side is where their own responsibilities, choices, needs and wants are. The game works by each player staying on their own side, respecting the boundary (the net) in the middle and engaging and interacting with another player who is also equally playing by the rules and staying on and taking care of their own side of the court. If we are over on the other persons side of the court, trying to control, taking care of their needs, justifying their actions, taking on their responsibility for their stuff, then the game simply does not work. It is the same for relationships. In order for healthy relationships to be enjoyed, you need to learn how to stay on your own side of the court, respect a healthy middle-ground boundary and not stray too far onto the other side. If you do, you interfere with all that is the other persons and that is not healthy. In fact, by doing so you can even play a very active part in preventing the other person from ever learning to or ever having to take responsibility for themselves and their actions. This is often seen in families of addicts or where there is mental health issues in the family or relationship. With addiction or mental health, and the same goes for narcissism, there is almost always invariably a parent or partner who will happily jump into an unhealthy codependent role, often straying over to the other persons side of the court to take on all the responsibilities of the other person. For parents or partners of addicts or alcoholics or narcissists this is done by making excuses for their bad behaviour, justifying abusive actions, supporting them financially, lying on their behalf, cleaning up their mess, taking care of their affairs and so on. This is what is happening any time you make excuses for or justify or down play what the narcissist does or says. This is also what is happening anytime you become more focused on what the narcissist in your life is doing or might do or wants or needs. Stop. Your responsibility needs to be much more with attending to *your own* wants and needs. This is not selfish. This is necessary. Attend to your own choices that you are making. You are responsible for you.

Reflection point:

* If you had to honestly and objectively position where you have been or currently are in terms of focus, attention, sense of control, responsibility and care, where would you place yourself on the court? Are you on your side of the court? Looking at and taking care of your own needs, looking at your own actions, and all that is your responsibility?

- ✷ Or are you somewhere over the other side? Over-concerned or over-involved in what others might want or need or what is going on over there? On what a narcissistic partner or family member might do or is doing now?
- ✷ What is happening when you find yourself drifting over to the other side?
- ✷ How does it feel to be on the wrong side of the court?
- ✷ What is it like to stay on your side and to keep the focus on yourself?

The other side is not within your control, it is not your business and it is certainly not your responsibility. Learn to prioritise, to take care of, and stay on your own side first and foremost. Let the others manage theirs. That is how the game is played. That is how healthy, fulfilling relationships are enjoyed.

HOW TO SET A BOUNDARY

Setting boundaries first of all takes tuning into your inner sense of self. Boundaries reflect our values and what is important to us. It takes listening to and taking notice of all the messages and communication we have within ourselves – our feelings, our gut instinct, our felt-sense. More often than not, we have disconnected from this along the way, perhaps we ignore or deny our inner truth. Many people override their gut instinct with their intellect. Knowing your boundaries is helped by sensing into what *feels* right for you. It's an inner knowing that you can absolutely trust. Our minds tell us all sorts of nonsense, but our inner knowing comes from a deeper place – it's not just cognitive.

Setting boundaries also requires some assertiveness, self-confidence, esteem and self-worth. It may well be daunting if this is new to you, however one of the wonderful things about working on developing healthier boundaries is that by doing so will in itself support the development of these characteristics. They are all interrelated. It's simply about getting started. Small steps and you build from there.

Having boundaries relies on having a sense of your own values. It can be helpful to consider the following questions:

* What is important to me?
* How do I want to live my life?
* What are my limits?
* What qualities do I value, e.g. trust,honesty, respect.
* What personal qualities do I admire or aspire to?
* What do I like?
* What don't I like?
* What annoys or irritates me?
* How would I like things to be?

Reflection point:

* What fears or concerns do I have about setting boundaries, if any?
* Take some time to think about what is important to you. What are your values?
* What do you want from others in relationships?
* What is not OK for you in relationships?
* What are absolute deal-breaker behaviours for you?
* How do you like to treat others?
* How do you expect others to treat you?
* Is there any difference between the two? If so, why?
* What would it mean to you to state your boundary or to say 'no'.
* What would it give you to be able to do that?
* Know that whatever positive that is, that you deserve that. Also know that you are the person responsible for giving yourself that.
* What might it be like to assert your boundary?

COMMUNICATING BOUNDARIES

The first step with boundaries is recognising within yourself first and foremost what your values and limits are. What is OK for you? What is not? Getting irritated or angry by certain things are usually a good indicator that something is pushing on a boundary of yours. Your feelings are one way to help you identify your limits and to help establish your boundaries. The clearer you are about your feelings, values and worth, then the easier it is for you to be clearer about them with other people. Setting boundaries means making it clear to others what is acceptable for you and what is not. This can be done as clearly and directly as you feel comfortable with or as is necessary.

1. Communicate clearly

One key to communicating boundaries is to stop believing you or anybody else can communicate telepathically. Please do not expect anybody to somehow miraculously be able to mind read or know what it is you want or don't want without you telling them. We cannot communicate in this way and believing we can is dangerous and unhealthy. This kind of fantasy thinking absolutely sets us up for suffering – one that we cause for ourselves. It is not other peoples responsibility to somehow know, or to spend their time trying to guess or work out what it is you are thinking, what you want or don't like or what your boundaries are. Just as it is not your responsibility to attempt to do that for anybody else. Be clear in your communications, words and actions. When this is mutually reciprocated it makes for very straightforward, clear, honest and healthy relationships. Keep it simple.

2. Boundaries have consequences

Having clear boundaries also involves thinking about the consequences of what you will do or what will happen, should that line be stepped over by anyone (which will happen). When you affirm your boundaries, you are aiming to make it clear to the other person what your preferences are as well what the consequences are for any deviations from that. For example, it is no use just saying *"I don't want you to cheat on me..."* A narcissist most likely will. A firm and clear boundary in a relationship says; *"Infidelity is an absolute NO for me (because I value trust and monogamy) and if you ever cheat I will leave"*. Notice the consequence is about something that *you* will action. Boundaries are not about trying to control or change the other person. It's about you and what you are going to do.

Communicating boundaries and subsequent consequences can be done very simply and firmly in a way that serves to mark the parameters for all parties involved. Affirming boundaries and stating clear consequences is much like how you might assert yourself with a child. (Remember a narcissist is basically a toddler!) You may say to a child *"tidy your room and then you can go out to play with your friends... If you don't tidy your room then I won't let you out to play"*. The expectation, your wants and the consequence is clear.

3. Boundaries are firm

An essential part of boundary holding is being able to stay firm with them and the consequences. That means if the child does not tidy their room, you have said they will not be allowed out. That *has* to mean that they are not going out. Irrespective of how much whining, pleading, crying, manipulating, screaming and so on that may be thrown at you. If you back down and give in anyway, you are simply showing them that what you say means nothing. That there are no rules. That you have no boundaries. Similarly, if your boundary is that, for example, cheating is a no, and you've stated you will leave if there is any infidelity, then you must stay firm to your boundary and consequence and end the relationship. Firm boundaries mean not getting swayed by any attempts of manipulation.

Visualise the tiny naughty toddler in the narcissist – Many clients I work with find it helpful to visualise the narcissistic partner or person as a small child. In some sense, that is pretty much what a narcissist is anyway. Think about holding boundaries with them as you would a small child. All children absolutely need boundaries. They look for them. They respond to them. It is in their benefit – as well as yours – to have healthy, firm boundaries. They may well test them at times, but this is to check they are held. Firm boundaries create safety and containment – this is what young children are testing for when they push boundaries. As with toddlers, naturally, you can expect some resistance or retaliation but still, you know that the best thing is to stay firm and maintain your boundary. This is for their benefit as much as it yours. It is so important to. Otherwise, what do children learn? They learn ways to manipulate in order to get what they want. Just like a narcissist does. When the narcissist next pushes your boundary, try to visualise them as a toddler having a tantrum. They will want to resist, fight, scream, throw their toys around, but just as you may with a toddler, simply calmly reiterate the boundaries. Do not allow the toddler to divert you away from your rules or to get their own way out of childish tantrum behaviours.

Crucially, you learning what *your* boundaries are and then stating them, as well as what you will do as a consequence of that boundary being tested, is a wonderful way of you staying on your side of the court. This is not about trying to control others. If you are trying to control or manipulate what others do then realise you have drifted onto their side of the court. You are in the wrong place! Get back to your side and stay there. Focus on and stay on your side along with what is true to you. Stay in touch with what you want and need and all that is your responsibility. This is not selfish. This is being a responsible adult. Doing so importantly gives the other person the space to learn, the space to take responsibility for themselves and to take care of all that is their own – should they so wish. The subsequent boundary that is created separates any unhealthy enmeshments. This is the difference between *interdependence* (healthy, adult, emotionally mature and respectful relationships) and *codependence* (dysfunctional and damaging relationships).

With healthy boundaries it is OK that other people may disagree with or be upset by your choices or opinions. It is fine that one person can be OK and the other person isn't. The boundary serves to separate the differences between the two. Boundaries have consequences. It is a crucial part of recovery to learn what your own boundaries are and how to state and hold them. This means being clearer about what's important to you, your needs and wants. It takes healthy and clear communication about those things. It requires thinking ahead to the consequences of what actions *you* will take if your boundaries are crossed and finally, it then takes sticking to them, holding those boundaries firmly.

As a simple example, in my work, I cannot control when people want to get in touch with me. When people want to email or phone me is their business (that's their side of the court). It is not my responsibility. It is not within my control. I could potentially drive myself crazy trying to control this. I can't. However, what *is* within my control and is my responsibility is when I choose to pick up and respond to messages and how I communicate that. This means me stating clearly to people my boundaries regarding when I will check my email or phone. I do not check work messages in the evening or at the weekends. This is because I value my family and free time. They are important to me. It is also important to manage expectations all round. So in making my boundary clear, I simply let people know that I do not check my messages at those times. That does not and will not stop people from contacting me during those times, that is not the aim. That is their choice and their responsibility – it is not about me trying to control or even focus on what other people are doing. Your healthy boundaries focus on what you are doing. The consequence in my case, is that they will not get a reply from me during those times. I am clear about the expectations. My responsibility is managing my own boundaries and my actions. What other people do in response to that is theirs. Equally, if I stated in my boundaries that I do not respond to emails at the weekend but then go ahead and do that, what kind of message does that give? Boundaries and consequences need to be clear and importantly, whatever they are you need to stick to them.

Another fairly common example of this is the demanding boss who asks or expects us to stay working late too often. We find this irritating as we'd clearly rather get off home and do other things. This reflects what is important to us. We may have other interests we'd much rather be doing, even if that includes not doing much at all! This again, reflects our values. But if we find saying 'no' difficult then we find ourselves reluctantly staying on. We may feel increasingly resentful about it. By not being able to state our boundary clearly we may even be in danger of setting the scene for further expectations. Our boss and colleagues may get to see that we are somebody who will always take on what is asked of us, even if it is above and beyond realistic expectations. They get to learn that we are somebody that never says 'no'. It is a dangerous and self-fulfilling set-up of expectations, inability to hold a boundary and a fuel to further resentments and anger. You can see how a lack of boundary in this instance can very quickly escalate all sorts of knock-on issues. All the more reason to keep it simple and assert your boundaries. So it is important to learn boundaries and in particular consider what may be the feelings that get in the way of us being able to state and hold them. It is usually fear or guilt. If that is the case, then this identifies issues to be worked through and to be let go of.

A MODEL FOR COMMUNICATING
BOUNDARIES

One solid basis for healthy communication and boundary setting
in general is to state something along the lines of:

*"When you do A (an action, behaviour or comment), it makes
me feel B (emotion / feeling). And I don't like it. So from now
on, if/when you do A again, I will do X (action = leave, end the
communication, etc).*

*adapt this to suit your own communication style.

I would like to point out something important here specifically
in relation to narcissists. Generally speaking, giving somebody
else feedback into how their actions impact you (B) can be a
helpful and healthy discussion to have. This is simply because
some people are not always so aware of how they are coming
across and therefore it's important and helpful feedback to
have. For most people, this would have an immediate and
positive impact in helping others to be more considerate and if
appropriate, alter their behaviours in a way that doesn't have
such a negative or detrimental impact. A lot of people would
appreciate feedback. Of course there are ways of delivering
this. Usually this is best done sensitively and considerately
rather than harshly, punitively or in a way that is judgemental
or shaming. Either way, in some circumstances, and especially
with narcissists, it may be that the behaviour won't change or
stop and so it's for you to manage how *you* will then respond to
that. That is your responsibility. When dealing with somebody
with a narcissistic personality disorder or a socio or psychopath,
including the B part of the above sentence can possibly be like
spoon-feeding the narcissist with your vulnerabilities. For
some particularly abusive individuals, knowing that certain
behaviours of theirs may make you feel frightened or guilty or

upset, will be great news for them. In the mind of a narcissist, they will simply be making a mental note as to what gets to you and then use it accordingly in an abusive way to manipulate in the future. I include it in the above example to give you an idea of what can be helpful in healthy relationships. You may need to consider carefully if you share your emotional feelings with the narcissist in your life or not. Narcissists generally don't care too much about how you feel or worse still when they use it to manipulate for they own gains.

To give you some other examples of this communication protocol, it could be something like:

"When you raise your voice to me, it makes me feel very uncomfortable and anxious. I don't like it. So from now on, if you raise your voice to me again, I am going to leave, remove myself from the situation and I will only talk to you again when you are able to talk in a calm, respectful way".

Or more directly:

"It is not OK to raise your voice at me like that. If you do, I will not speak to you again until you can talk about things in a more appropriate and calm way."

Or simply:

"Don't talk to me like that. That is not OK."

Perhaps you can see with each of the three examples, an increase in confidence, self-assurance and directness in boundary setting. Simultaneously there is also less fear or guilt. Notice also that the consequence reflects an action of what *you* will do or not do. Sometimes a simple and clear *'No, this is not OK'* is more than enough – no need for an explanation or consequence. Go with whatever feels right for you. Remember though, one of the most important thing in setting boundaries is sticking to them.

STEP-BY-STEP PROCESS OF SETTING A BOUNDARY:

1. Recognise in yourself what your boundaries are. What are your values? Identify what your limits are. What is OK or not OK for you? Be clear in yourself about this first.
2. Communicate this clearly and directly to others.
3. Know and/or state what the consequence will be if your boundary is not respected.
4. Stand strong and stick to your boundaries and any related consequences.

MAINTAIN THE FOCUS

As mentioned in the previous chapter, those that have a problem with you setting boundaries are usually those that benefit from you having none. Those sorts of people will most likely kick back against any boundaries you set. That is their choice. It's their side of the court. It's their responsibility. That's not your responsibility or within your control. Recovery is absolutely about re-shifting the focus back to you and all that is within your control as well as what is your responsibility.

A boundary serves a number of helpful and important functions. It communicates your values. It reflects self-respect and integrity. Boundaries are an essential part of a healthy relationship. Boundaries also go hand-in-hand with our sense of self worth and esteem.

Many people who experience difficulties in setting boundaries identify with being a people-pleaser or are overly care-taking. In other words, have an over-sense of responsibility for other peoples mood, emotions or behaviour. There may be some deep or early anxiety about the other persons reaction that interfere with an ability or view of boundary setting. But you must remember, the other persons reaction is *their* responsibility. You can't control that. It is not your job to. Healthy boundary setting is about being clear around what is your responsibility and what is not. Your responsibility is for what you say and how you say it. That is your side of the court. You are not responsible for what somebody hears or for how they want to interpret the information. You are also not responsible for how they react. That is *their* responsibility. That is happening on *their* side of the court. The boundary (net) remains in between and marks where your side begins and ends, as well as where the other side begins and ends. Leave them to it and stay focused on your side. Anytime you notice you are over the other side, simply refocus and return to you and your side.

Healthy boundaries are set in a calm, assertive, gentle yet firm and fair manner. It's not a power struggle. In time, as you experiment with and develop your sense of boundary you may become aware of feelings that interrupt or interfere with your ability to state of hold boundaries firmly. Some people may fear an aggressive response, abandonment or rejection. Some people feel guilty as if they are responsible for the other person. It may be that you can be aware of any fears or guilt and that is OK. Awareness in itself can be enough for change. Feelings of fear or guilt can exist, and you be mindfully aware of those feelings, yet are still able to communicate and hold your boundaries. Try to let go of fear or guilt. If you find however that you are experiencing enough fear or guilt that it significantly interferes with your ability to set and maintain healthy boundaries for yourself then I would encourage you to find an understanding psychotherapist or psychologist to help more specifically with this. It may be that there are past experiences or specifically, past traumas where this has been too difficult or overwhelming for you and getting the right kind of support can help you specifically to work through them. Therapy can help you to let go of fear and guilt or anything else that interferes with your ability to hold healthy boundaries. Anything that gets in the way of you having healthy boundaries is going to get in the way of you enjoying healthy relationships. Seek professional support to help with anything that gets in the way of you being able to learn and enjoy all that comes from having healthier boundaries. This can be hugely positive and a very kind, loving thing to do for yourself. Therapy can be a wonderful gift and a worthwhile investment for this kind of thing. It is helpful and you are worth it.

KEY POINTS:

* You are entitled to have boundaries. Everybody is.
* Boundaries are about knowing yourself, knowing what you value and what is important to you.
* Healthy relationships rely on healthy boundaries.
* Healthy boundaries are a crucial part of self-care.
* We are all responsible for setting and stating our own boundaries.
* We are not responsible for other peoples.
* Clear boundaries have clear consequences.
* We should respect other peoples boundaries.
* Other people should respect ours.
* You absolutely have the right to express your wants and needs in an appropriate way.
* It is your responsibility to attend to and take care of your own wants and needs.
* You are entitled to your feelings. Every single one of them.
* We can let go of any old, inaccurate or unhelpful messages we may have grown up with about boundaries and self-care.

* Boundaries and self-esteem go hand in hand.
* Developing boundaries goes alongside developing self-confidence, self-esteem and self-worth.
* Your boundaries are about your limits, your values, your wants. Your boundaries are about you. Keep the focus on you.

Reflection point:

In practical terms, it can be a good idea to start with setting small manageable boundaries to sense into what that feels like for you and anything that brings up for you.

* What are your concerns about that, if any?
* What does it feel like to set a boundary?
* What was your family message around boundaries and self care?
* What boundaries do you think you could set now?

---

18.   Communicating with a narcissist

Communicating with a narcissist, when unarmed with the necessary tools, can be completely and utterly maddening. At best it can feel like you are talking completely different languages. Narcissists have a need to, and will want to control communication with others. They will likely only ever want to talk when it suits them and even then be particular and controlling about what it is discussed.

As everything is about them, narcissists will tend to quite happily chatter away endlessly about themselves. If they are more of an overt type of narcissist, this could include how wonderful they are, or if more covert, whatever may be the latest issues, fall outs, or dramas they are going through. Narcissists usually have a lot to say about their latest achievements, special treatments, how great they are, or how troubled they are and how well or how badly they have been treated by others recently. Narcissists actively seek contact with others who will listen to this patiently and non-judgementally, be engaged and in awe of or interested in all they have to say about themselves. This person is typically the silent, lost voice echoist-type who is more comfortable listening to others than speaking up themselves. Narcissists rarely ask how you are or are interested in listening to you. If they do, it is fleeting and insincere or to serve their own selfish needs. It is not unheard of for narcissists to sit and talk non-stop for shockingly long periods of time. It can leave anybody coming away from a meeting wondering if next time they might get a chance to speak!

Narcissists demand and command space in relationships. They can be very dominant in their communication style, often coming across quite aggressive, threatening or intimidating. One particularly harsh way narcissists control communication is to simply cut it off completely. This is again, on their terms, for as long as they want, when it suits them. Such silent treatment communicates a message about who they believe holds power. This kind of communication is in itself a form of emotional abuse. The cut-off can often be highly anxiety-provoking and distressing to the recipients and is by design utilised for that purpose. It is simply another way a narcissist will attempt to hold power and control over others.

COMMON WAYS IN WHICH NARCISSISTS COMMUNICATE INCLUDE:

* Silent treatment. Suddenly cutting contact. Blocking your contact and/or social media. They often reappear when they feel like it too and expect people to be ready and willing to engage in communication with them again, usually as if nothing has happened and expecting full forgiveness and forgetfulness.
* Blatant direct verbal abuse and bullying, name calling, shouting, screaming, narcissist rage, blaming, shaming and threatening.
* Withholding information. The narcissist maintains a sense of power and control by purposely withholding information.
* Intrigue. Similar to withholding information but with teasing you with snippets of information or making comments designed to trigger your intrigue and interest.

* **Projecting.** Accusing you or others of all that they themselves are. Classic examples are: *"Look at how angry you are!"*, *"You are not reliable"*, *"You are a narcissist!"*
* **Lying.**
* Being judgemental and critical.
* Narcissists are often terrible gossips. They will gossip and spread slander and lies.
* Topping. For example, if you earn a certain amount, they earn more. You have just taken up jogging they have already run six marathons.
* Drip-feeding. Otherwise known as 'bread-crumbing'. This is when pieces of information are drip-fed intentionally and teasingly. Specifically with the aim of creating a reaction, mostly intrigue and anxiety.
* 'Pocketing' or Splitting. This is when a narcissist 'pockets' people within a group. It means to purposefully step in as the middle-man communicator between others. It splits people off from one another. This stops and interrupts people having any clear or direct communication with each other. This is something the narcissist may find threatening and has a need to be in control of. Again, it is another way of controlling and manipulating relationships. This can also create a perfect opportunity for a narcissist to stir conflict and issues between others (see also 'drama triangle').
* Inconsistencies. Narcissists are consistently inconsistent in what they say and do.
* Finger-pointing. Rather than take responsibility for themselves or offer clarity about their own actions, they will simply point fingers about what you or anybody else is doing or not doing. This is designed to then throw people into a defensive position and take away any negative attention or potential criticism away from themselves. Finger-pointing can also support the view that they are the victim.

* Bomb-throwing. Usually to avoid any negative attention or having to take any responsibility for their actions, narcissists they will throw in completely and utterly irrelevant bombs into the conversation to distract and deter others away from the current subject.

Another particular communication behaviour narcissists utilise is something I call 'fishing'. I find it helpful and so I also try to encourage clients I work with to imagine the narcissist as a fisherman. In fact, I like to visualise them as one of those funny looking little garden gnomes sitting on a toadstool with a pointy hat and a fishing rod. The narcissistic-gnome will throw his or her fishing rod in your direction and try all sorts of different bait in order to catch you and get you to bite. They will be skilled in recognising the most likely kind of bait you might go for.

Increasing your mindful awareness of this as it happens can be a key help in breaking the cycle of automatically biting at the bait that is thrown your way. In practical steps, this means to:

1. **Arm yourself with information:** Learn and inform yourself about the typical narcissistic communication techniques.

Both in general, and more specific to the person or people in your life.

2. **Identify:** Identifying the kind of bait they use to try to pull you in or affect you in anyway.

3. **Name the bait:** Label it for yourself. (eg. *guilt-tripping, financial incentive, criticism, intrigue-provoking*). Labelling the bait can help take the power out of it. It helps to make this clear.

4. **Recognise what the bait stirs up in you:** Does it trigger you to feel anxious, panicky, guilty or responsible?

5. **Recognise your bait vulnerabilities:** Recognise what kind of 'bait' triggers you, or most likely affects you, tempts you, pulls you back to the narcissist, pushes against your boundary, or forces a collapse in your boundary. Get to know what your vulnerabilities are in this kind of communication dynamic.

6. **Prepare yourself:** Armed with the above information you can then better prepare yourself. Perhaps you can even begin to predict the bait the fisherman-narcissist will try and throw your way. Being able to predict the use of bait absolutely takes the power out of it. We are less likely to be caught off guard with it too. As you become more and more aware of this happening, the broader perspective in itself can help you maintain distance and to not be pulled in or affected negatively. Try to maintain the focus on what his or her words or comments throw up inside of you and just notice that. What are the feelings? Breath, slow down. Take some time.

7. **Bring the focus back to you:** Take your time. Give your self some space. Bring the focus back to you. Attend to your own needs in response to the above. Rather than reacting or otherwise giving the narcissist what they want, stay close to what it is you need for you in that moment.

Narcissists thrive on emotional reactions in other people and so they inherently attempt to provoke them in any which way they can.

Some techniques or 'bait' used, in addition to the above, includes:

* **Intrigue.** Classic narcissistic-fishing technique of trying to pull in and attract interest in their target. This will involve offering some small snippet of vague or intriguing piece of information or comment in the hope that it will pull you into ask more questions due to intrigue and/or anxiety.

* **False accusations.** A narcissist is looking for a reaction simply in order to have you or anybody else engage with them. False accusations are an easy way to try and do this as a natural immediate response is for people to want to quickly defend themselves. Nobody likes to be blamed wrongly. However, try to simply identify this for what it is. Bait. The strength comes for *you* when *you* can identify this as bait and then resist your urge to bite or be pulled into a defensive position. Let go of your need to explain or justify. A narcissist will believe whatever it is they want and their version of you or things anyway! Leave them to it.

* **Guilt-tripping.** Feelings of guilt can be triggered that cause a collapse in personal boundaries. Let go of guilt. A narcissist is accountable. Don't bite the bait and leave them to it.

* **Being a victim.** In order to elicit sympathy, empathy and understanding. Sometimes a narcissist will play being a victim in order to have others feel for them. They aim to pull people into a care-taking or fixing position.

* **Analysis paralysis.** Narcissists will want to and even demand to 'talk' about the relationship. This is another indulgence that is used as bait to pull somebody into a discussion or argument. Please note: people in healthy relationships rarely spend time analysing or discussing it – they are far too busy simply enjoying said relationship. Overanalyses of the 'relationship' is a sign in itself that it is unhealthy.

* **Being argumentative or provocative.** Deliberately trying to start a fight. Don't bite the bait.
* **Pulling on heart strings.** Similar to guilt-tripping but looking to elicit empathy and sympathy.
* **Over-bearing care and concern for you or others.** Invading your personal boundaries by stating or behaving as over-concerned or over-responsible. Not respecting your wishes for space or silence. This is controlling and usually a starting point to then shifting the conversation and focus back to them and/or provoking an argument.
* **Name calling / verbal abuse.** Saying intentionally provocative things with the intention of pushing your buttons and eliciting a reaction.
* **Team play abuse.** This is where the narcissist will bring onside other peoples view or opinions (whether it's true or not) in order to provoke you. This is usually mixed with intrigue. Such as "They were right about you... I knew I should have listened to them..." Without any further elaboration, this is abusive and cruel and designed to create anxiety and upset.
* **Manipulation.** Includes a confusing and conflicting mix of compliments, gifts and abuse.
* **The silent treatment.**
* **Direct threats.**
* **Love-bombing.** Declarations and demonstrations of 'love'.
* **False-hope.** This is the dangling of the carrot on a string specifically about what they know you may want in life, such as to have a child or a financial or lifestyle purchase or situation. The fantasy and hope of them providing you with or helping you with this is used as bait.

Recognise the bait tactics for simply what they are and resist biting. You can learn to stop snapping at the bait when you focus more on recognising and attending to your own needs. Don't take whatever the narcissist does or say personally and leave them to it. I worked with a narcissistic colleague once who used to pass very intriguing and vague comments to me about what other colleagues had supposedly said. They would say things like *"well that person has their own view about you..."*, or *"they warned me about you"*. It triggered some anxiety and intrigue in me in the beginning. Nobody likes to think people are saying unpleasant things about them. He would then refuse to elaborate or explain further. But his random comments were relentless. It was enough to leave you feeling paranoid and mistrusting. I recognised that this was what he would do with other people though. It really caused disharmony and distrust in the group but I could see it was his way of controlling. As soon as I recognised that, I saw the bait and stopped biting. Whenever he would say comments that were designed to elicit intrigue or anxiety I would not let it – because I could see it for what it was. Bait and his way of trying to control. So then I would just reply *"oh ok, well they can think whatever they want"*, *"OK, that's up to them'*, *"OK, thanks"*. I don't actually believe anyone else was even saying anything at all but that wasn't the point – I had stopped giving him any reaction. I'd stopped having any reaction – because I could see that it was just his fishing attempts! I can't say for sure it stopped him doing it, but for me, I had stopped biting and so it no longer had any affect on me. That's one of the reasons why I can't recall for sure if he stopped as *I* had just stopped noticing or caring! Therefore it didn't matter. I left him to it.

For a narcissist, any kind of emotional reaction they can illicit in others is a twisted way in which they manage to feel better about themselves. Whilst you or anybody else is reacting strongly to them, they are reinforcing the message that *they* have power and control. You can regain this sense of control for yourself and subsequently change the relationship dynamic by learning to manage your own emotional reactions and responses around them. That is not to say you will not have any, but you don't need to show them, share them or let them know or see that. All the whilst a narcissist continues to know they can affect you in one way or another, they will continue to do so. They will continue to provoke. The moment you can consistently take that away from them is the moment you alter the power dynamic. You regain control.

COMMUNICATION TIPS:

Going 'No Contact':

Many people ask about going 'no contact'. My simple advice is: **If there is any possibility that you can completely cut contact with a narcissist, then do it.** Your mental health will rarely be enhanced by being in relationship with narcissists so if there is any chance you can cut this out then do it. There may be some aftereffect, 'hangover' to cutting contact, and maybe even a process of grief, but you can use the suggestions outlined throughout this book to continue to bring the focus back to your own self-care and what you need in order to recovery and move through any of that. Focus on developing healthier friendships and relationships with other people and enjoy your own interests and pursuits. It gets easier in time and is ultimately the healthiest thing you can do for yourself.

It is worth noting that if you do decide to cut contact then by doing so, there will be a period of time where the dynamic in the relationship shifts. When you cut contact, you are regaining control. A narcissist will rarely appreciate that. When you do, you may then observe the narcissist trying every which way they can possibly come up with, to try and provoke some reaction or contact from you. I have seen many people fall back into contact and then re-entering the toxic relationship because of this. This can happen again and again with a narcissist and is how the relationship can continue for years. Please do not fall into some fantasy trap about what that might mean. This stage is simply a game of power for a narcissist. For them, it will just be about a battle of wit. To some extent, it doesn't even matter what the reaction or form of contact from you might be. It only matters that there is one. If you decide to go no contact, don't give them any contact. At all. It has to be consistent. Equally, many times the reaction of the narcissist is to cut you out and to insist, gossip and believe that this was their choice and their decision. If that is the case, let them get on with it. What they want to believe or say is their side of the court, it is their business, their responsibility and their choice. What you and anybody else wants to believe or say is yours. Let them have their own version of reality. Trying to change that is out of your control and will only likely bring you distress and suffering. Focus on you and moving forward.

Remember that narcissists are essentially gambling addicts. In many ways, just like a gambler, they are constantly hedging their bets as to who can bring the best narcissistic supply for them at any given time. Also, just like a gambling addict, they will be hooked in by the occasional pay out. A gambling addict can sit at the slot machine feeding money into it all day without a single win, spending thousands and simply not register his or her losses. The one win though, no matter how small or menial, is the thing that makes them feel like they have won. Any small victory keeps them hooked. When it comes to a narcissist, you are more likely to be the one to lose in terms of the emotional stress and trauma this kind of ongoing abusive relationship can cause. For a narcissist, they will try every manipulation tactic and variety of bait they can think of in order to provoke a reaction from you, or to get you to break no contact. You may see them try abusive tactics, love-bombing, promising the world, being aggressive, insulting, manipulative, flattering, feigning illness, trying to guilt-trip you, pulling on your heart strings and so on, the list is endless. Chances are, if you have known this narcissist for a while, they will know precisely which buttons of yours to press. You can stay strong with no contact by first of all simply being mindful and aware of this. Hopefully this comes from having read and studied much of what is written in this book so far, as well as practising techniques such as mindfulness and self-reflection. In time it will become easier and easier to not only recognise and see things for what they are, but to not even feel in the slightest bit inclined to respond or react. You can let it go. Time and space absolutely offers the perspective you need to move away, and ultimately stay away from toxic relationships.

If no contact is not an option, then you want to ideally try and **limit the contact you have as much as possible.** A narcissist again, will want to try and pull you into dialogue or any kind. Do not let them. This is your choice. They might hit a tennis ball over to your side of the court but it is up to you whether you want to knock it back and engage in play.

If you recognise a narcissist 'fishing' and trying to pull you in with bait, try and observe objectively what happens. Watch and name any techniques you spot that they try to utilise. For example; naming, shaming, pulling on heart strings, pointing fingers, guilt-tripping, crying, screaming, being aggressive, trying to provoke your anxiety and so on.

Watch what techniques they attempt and name them in your own mind for yourself.

Then observe your inner reaction. What is that like for you on the inside? How does it feel? What thoughts or feelings of yours do you notice?

Just notice this. Observe it. Name it.

Consider **what do I need?** Having recognised how you are feeling, then consider what it is you need in that moment? Attend to your own self-care needs. Focus on what is best for you for your own wellbeing and recovery. Ask yourself if any choice of yours is potentially harmful or healing for you?

Remember boundaries, focus on you and leave the narcissist to it.

The moment we become aware of what is happening, mindfully, objectively and non-judgementally is the moment we create some space. With space, we can then slow down and consider how we may wish to respond, rather than react.

If you have a situation where things are at a legal stage with a narcissist, for example, divorce or business litigation, if at all possible leave the contact to the professionals. Communicate with your legal team and let them deal with all correspondence.

Keep communication to an absolute minimum. A narcissist will try and pull you into a discussion or debate in order to serve their own needs and ultimately regain power. Do not let them. Be very, very short and direct in the communication from your side. Keep with a simple 'yes' or 'no' or 'don't know', or 'I will come back to you on that'. Try to resist any temptation to explain or elaborate. For example, when it comes to making arrangements for any childcare be direct and clear. "I will pick them up on Friday at 4pm". Full stop.

A narcissist will be hellbent on trying to derail any straight forward, healthy communication. Attempts to pull you in, change the subject and throw you off track can include:

* Being directly aggressive, insulting or argumentative.
* Refusing to speak / silent treatment.
* Trying to turn things around on you eg. *"well, if you didn't X, then I would not have had to do Y"*.
* Making suggestions that may trigger feelings of guilt, fear or paranoia for you.
* Gas-lighting.
* Finger pointing. Either trying to direct attention to you or others.

* Trying to shift attention on you. *"Look at how you are acting right now, listen to how you are talking"*, *"You are being aggressive"*, etc.
* Attempts to change the subject completely. They may attempt to throw even the most irrelevant, unrelated comments at you in an attempt to control and disrupt the conversation focus.

Watch and observe their attempts. This helps you to take a step back from it. Sit back and watch 'the narcissist show'. Their behaviours can be ridiculous to watch sometimes. Just watch. Detach. Then simply stay on track with your own communication and continue to speak in a very direct way as described above. There is no need for elaboration, discussion or argument. This is what they want. Don't let them throw you off track. In time, you may even find watching and identifying their array of attempts as being quite comical. When you can see these things for what they are – attempts to control – that already takes the power away.

One tool that you may find helpful when dealing with a narcissist is to **imagine them as the toddler** they more or less actually are. Narcissists are essentially stumped emotionally in some ways at a young age. If you have ever seen a narcissist in full rage you may recognise the toddler tantrum behaviour. Shouting, screaming, throwing things around, anything to get their way. When you see this in action, simply imagine them as a toddler and respond accordingly, just as you would when dealing with a child. When faced with a screaming and stroppy child, you probably would not let them upset you. You probably wouldn't let anything they say or do get to you. We don't take it personally. We see it for what it is... the child's mood in that moment. It is something we do not need and in fact, should not get pulled into. Instead we can stay calm, composed, detached and simply repeat whatever it is we want to communicate. We simply reinstate our boundaries.

Be clear in your intention for communication and do not get sidetracked. It can be helpful to consider before any contact with a narcissist what it is you specifically intend to get from the communication. Communication of any kind has a purpose. What information is it that you would like to get from this particular contact exchange? For example; To know will they be attending the meeting? What time are they picking up the kids? How much is owed?

There should be a clear, straightforward question with potential for a clear, straightforward answer.

With a clear agenda for specific information, you can much more easily stay on track. Keep in mind what it is you would like to get from the communication and do not allow them to sidetrack you or pull you off on a tangent or into any other kind of discussion, reflection or debate. When the narcissist then attempts to do so, which they will, simply ignore it. Repeat and reiterate your direct question. Stay focused. This allows you to corner them for a simple and direct answer. If, for whatever reason, they refuse or are unable to give you that, then simply state what is happening objectively. *"OK, I would like to know what time you are dropping the kids off at, but you are refusing to do that. I am asking you a question and you are refusing to give me a clear answer"*. Try not to do this in an accusatory way, instead keep it simple and objective. Do not make it personal or provocative. It's an objective observation. Importantly though, this helps you to mark a clear boundary about communication and responsibility. By being able to state things in this way, you communicate clearly what it is you want, as well as stating what it is they are saying or doing or not saying or not doing. This highlights to both parties who is responsible for each part of that communication. This is boundaries in action.

Give yourself time to respond. Another useful technique to consider is to be aware of giving yourself time. One of the techniques a narcissist will use is to pressure you to make a rash decision. You may not be ready to. You may need time to think about things and consider your options. Therefore, it can be really helpful to state that clearly. Such as simply; *"I'd like to have some time to think about that"* or *"I'll come back to you"*. This will likely infuriate a narcissist who will be trying to guilt-trip, gas-light or provoke anxiety and fear in you, in order to force you to make a decision they want, when they want it. Don't let them. You are well within your rights to take time to reflect on any decision. There is very rarely any situation with a narcissist where a decision of any kind needs to be made with absolute urgency. Bide your time. This can also be a helpful tool to utilise if you ever feel flustered in conversation with a narcissist. Stating you want time to think about things is a helpful way to give yourself that space and to bring whatever the topic is to a close for now. This is another way you can regain the control from your side of the communication.

The other vital component in healthy communication, as we have already covered in earlier chapters, is boundaries. State your boundary clearly, along with any consequences you have set and then *stick to them*. Narcissists struggle with healthy boundaries. They will likely want to challenge yours, no matter what they are. They will attempt to use their whole array of narcissistic manipulative tactics in order to do so. This can include anything from being vitriolic and abusive all the way through to being overly sweet, generous and seemingly 'helpful'. For example, they might try to make out they are doing you a favour in order to challenge and change your set boundaries. Watch our for this and do not let them. If you give them an inch, they will want a mile. For them, this stuff is a game. They want to just see that they have the power to ultimately get what they want, to have things their way, to have the sense of power and control that they win. Don't let them. Being completely consistent with boundaries is the quickest way to have them give up their hopes of continuing to abuse and manipulate and to get them to leave you alone and move on.

Of course, it helps to find ways to stay grounded and centred in yourself during these kinds of challenging conversations with a narcissist. Practicing ways to feel grounded and centred in yourself helps you to stay on point and to not get pulled or side-tracked onto something else. This can help you to stay focused in any attempts to have a more healthy, direct style of communication. It is also supportive to your boundaries.

COMMUNICATION TIPS IN SUMMARY

* If you can, go no contact.
* Keep communication to a minimum.
* Keep it simple. Keep it clear.
* Visualise the toddler in them.
* Visualise them as the fishing garden gnome, tossing out bait.
* Practice awareness – watch for the attempts of derailing the conversation and them bringing up something entirely different, random or throwing some other subject or attempt at insult into the mix.
* Be clear about what you want to discuss and be clear about what you don't and won't talk about.
* Stay focused.
* Give yourself time. Be willing to end any abusive discussion and walk away.
* Remember to hold firm boundaries with consequences.
* You are responsible for what you communicate. You are not responsible for what they hear, interpret or say.
* Return and refocus back to you. How you are feeling? What do you want? What do you need?

Reflection point:

* What has the communication pattern been like in the past? What do you recognise?
* How might you be able to improve or make changes to the way you communicate with a narcissist that is more helpful for you now and in the future?
* What are some of the bait techniques that you recognise? What is that like for you? What do you notice? How does it leave you feeling?
* What do you usually do?
* How does the focus and power usually drift back to the narcissist?
* How can you regain more control over that?
* What are some of the things, if any, that you worry may get in the way of that?
* What can you do to make this easier for you? What would help support you in better communication with a narcissist?
* Think about and prepare a few things you might say if you need to end any communication.

19.
Compassion & Forgiveness
– Softening our inner self-talk

I really wanted to make some points about the importance of compassion in particular, self-compassion as it is fundamental to recovery from narcissistic abuse and trauma. Many clients I see who have found themselves in relationships with narcissists, or have had a narcissistic parent or relative tend to have an alarmingly high tolerance level for stress and abuse. They also demonstrate a vast capacity for kindness, compassion and forgiveness when it comes to their abusive partner, family members, colleagues or anybody else yet in contrast are incredibly hard on themselves. They neglect their own wants and needs and have a highly punitive inner 'self-talk'.

Self-talk is the inner chatter we all have in our minds. It is our ingrained, automatic thinking. Our self-talk tends to develop from the sorts of things we have experienced, heard and been told during our early formative years. We develop our inner self-talk during our childhood, based on our direct experiences as well as picking up on the way, how our parents, teachers, friends and family speak to or about themselves, each other and us. We tend to absorb, much like a sponge, the voices of our parents, family and other caregivers. This may be positive, supportive and helpful or negative, unsupportive and unhelpful. This inner conversation is extremely powerful. It can be helpful or harmful. The words we use, including the language and tone, are the foundations for how we relate to ourselves, how we interact, how we think and feel and how we may grow and change. Although our internal self-talk comes from young and is ingrained early on, it can absolutely be changed. In recovery from narcissistic abuse, a kind, compassionate self-talk is essential for your own healing and growth. Honing a positive and supportive, loving, patient and kind self-talk is vital in your self care and in developing a healthy relationship with yourself.

It can be tricky to first begin to recognise your own internal chatter. It is something that is so automatic and habituated that we rarely notice, however it is something that affects us every day of our lives. We rarely tend to think about our thinking. Recognising our self-talk is not something we tend to learn at school or work either so this can take a bit of effort and practice in the beginning. You can start to notice your habitual self-talk by tuning into your thoughts and internal chatter. Practising 'mindfulness of thoughts' can help with this. This is where you just notice and observe your thoughts as if they were clouds passing by in the sky. Hopefully, by now, you would have had some practice at paying mindful attention to the breath in an objective non-judgemental way, in the present moment. Mindfulness of thoughts is bringing that practice to help notice whatever the thoughts are as they go through the mind. (See earlier chapter for 'mindfulness of thoughts' exercise). This is a very powerful and helpful practice in recognising and adapting your own self-talk.

It is common for people who find themselves experiencing narcissistic abuse or trauma to have harsh and punitive self-talk. Often, many people struggle to recognise just how hard they are being on themselves because it is a way of being they are simply so used to. Especially when a harsh or critical self-talk is a continuation of what was heard from parents or family or as we were growing up – it all becomes fairly normalised. We don't notice this is not helpful. The critical, punitive and negative internal voice tells us we aren't good enough, or that anything we do is not enough. It says we should be doing more, earning more, working more, eating less, drinking less, that we should be slimmer, prettier, stronger... That we should be able to do this, do that, be over it by now, be unaffected, that we shouldn't feel how we feel... It's the first to say that we messed up, remind us that we didn't do it right, that it is our fault... and so on. This kind of inner dialogue can drive us to push on, to keep going, to achieve and to do better. However, dangerously, if out of balance, negative, punitive self-talk can be a huge factor in manifesting perfectionism, low self-esteem, low self-worth, depression, anxiety, panic, obsessive-compulsive behaviours, addictions, eating disorders, stress and burn-out. Crucial to know is that this way of being is attractive to a narcissist as well as being a hindrance factor in recovery from narcissistic abuse.

Having a harsh, punitive inner self-talk is actually something that is often a part of the mentality of over-achievers and those who are very driven, ambitious or goal-focused. The incredibly driven "nothing but the best" type attitude often fuels drive, success and achievement. There are lots of material, financial and status gains to be made from this way of being. However it can fuel insecurities and issues with self-esteem. When this way of being becomes rigid and there is no let up from it, it can be the very thing that fuels addictive behaviour and elusive thinking of *"when I get X, then I will be happy or can slow down"*. That is the essence of fantasy, addictive thinking. It can create much discontentment, disappointment and frustration. Often when we are so advanced at being driven and achievement-oriented, it is to the neglect of developing a kind, gentle and compassionate inner self-talk. The same can be said for being in an abusive relationship. The words and actions of a narcissistic partner or parent can further absorb into our own internal punitive, unkind self-talk. It tells us that it is 'me' and 'my' fault, the belief that I'm the one with the issues, and if only I could do things differently, do better, be better, do more, be more… then everything will be fine. A critical or punitive self-talk needs to be addressed and modified to one that is much kinder, compassionate and gentle. It is a fundamental in recovery from narcissistic abuse and trauma. Usually when we have so much drive, this is in the absence of a kind, gentle, supportive and compassionate tone. Some people I work with actually fear that if they start to develop a kinder self-talk, all drive and ambition will immediately disappear and they will become completely lazy and gain 200lbs overnight from utter lack of motivation or activity! I can assure you that is highly unlikely. What is helpful and important though, is to address this imbalance between drive and self-care to one that is more balanced. That does not necessarily mean your work ethic and motivations suddenly disappear, but ideally it will help you approach goals and achievements with a much healthier balance and perspective. This is one where you can still achieve all you want to but in a way where you are more able to take care of your own needs rather than neglect them. Importantly, developing a kinder, more forgiving, supportive and compassionate self-talk helps us to make better decisions based on what is right for us. It helps us to do more of what is loving and good for us. We end up making healthier choices for ourselves when this fundamental is right. It also supports our recovery as we are able to respond to our experience, our needs and ourselves in a more understanding and compassionate manner. If you have experienced narcissistic abuse of any kind, chances are you've already been through more than enough. Don't keep adding fuel to the fire by continuing to beat yourself up or be hard on yourself. Long-term recovery and healing comes from learning to truly love yourself and this is reflected in your internal chatter.

In recovery we are seeking to turn the volume *down* on the harsh critic and instead turn the volume *up* on the kinder, more supportive 'best friend'.

Reflection point:

Using mindfulness or awareness-of-thought practices, try to notice your automatic self-talk as you go about each day. What are the automatic thoughts that go through your mind when you make a mistake, are late, or drop something? What thoughts do you have about yourself regarding where you are in your life right now? What are your thoughts and self-talk when you feel anxious or stressed? What is the tone of those automatic thoughts? Are they kind, supportive and reassuring? Or harsh and scalding? Notice how automatic this can be. Remember thoughts are not facts.

As you identify your harsh self-talk, ask yourself: *Would I speak to a close friend like this? Is this what I would say to somebody I really cared about?* If it's not, then ask yourself why would you speak to yourself in any other way? Why would you be kinder and friendlier to somebody else, than you are to yourself? The next, and perhaps most pivotal step then is to begin to talk to yourself in a caring, supportive, kind, compassionate, forgiving and reassuring way. Chances are you know how to be kind and caring. Most people who experience narcissistic abuse do. You are probably very good at being forgiving and understanding and supportive of others. Now it is time to fine-tune these skills and apply them to yourself. Be compassionate to yourself. Learn to be your own best friend.

SELF-COMPASSION IN PRACTICE

To recap, we usually learn and develop our inner self-talk during childhood and adolescence. We tend to inherit this from parents, caregivers or family members. We can also inherit our family values, beliefs and absorb the various messages we receive during our formative years about ourselves, others, the world we live in, about drive, work ethic, self-care, responsibility, blame and shame. Some of us end up being very driven in a bid to escape our family backgrounds and strive for something different, something better. Even the slightest neglectful or negative family background is enough to send somebody into full on survive and drive mode. Nothing so wrong with that. In many ways, being very driven, operating from a rational, logical part of our brains serves many helpful functions. It becomes a helpful resource that can support positive life change. With a focus that is much more on achievement, getting good grades, getting the 'right job', earning, climbing the career ladder, status, it helps us get things done, we progress. Being highly driven, uber-focused, somewhat detached, rational or otherwise 'heady' keeps us away from our feelings. When we are operating in logic and rationale, we are rarely in touch with the emotional parts of ourselves. And when the emotional parts have, at some point, been too overwhelming, too much, too frightening or too unpleasant... coming up into our heads, and developing a way of being that is *go, go, go,* or *do, do do,* complete with endless to-do lists and the like, serves a variety of very helpful and much appreciated functions at that time. However, I really want to emphasise, that the downside is that this leaves us out of touch with our emotional, felt-sense, our gut instinct and a compassionate part of ourselves and *that* leaves us vulnerable to narcissists. This is one of the reasons why working to balance out drive and compassion-to-self is so imperative. We have perhaps inherited ideas or at least learned along the way to put others first. We develop advanced skills in caring for others and attending to other people wants and needs whilst negating and neglecting our own feelings or needs. This is not healthy. There needs to be a balance.

So what does it really mean to have self-compassion? It's reflective of the inner dialogue we have. Our inner self-talk resides in our mind. It shapes our thinking and represents the relationship we have with ourselves. This inner voice has usually developed during childhood having absorbed, much like a sponge, the sorts of things we have heard others say to us, or have heard our parents, primary caregivers, siblings, family, teachers, friends and so on say to each other or about other people.

What kind of chatter, messages and beliefs have you
absorbed from your earlier years? Was it a harsh, critical
judgemental voice, or a kind, supportive tone?
Does your internal voice remind you of anyone?
Does it sound like somebody you know?
How do you ideally want to talk and relate to yourself?

Lots of us automatically insist we do love ourselves and have good self-esteem and can self-care and look after ourselves. But I invite you to seriously explore and investigate this further. You may be surprised. I believe there is almost always room for improvement. Fostering a kinder inner relationship and self-talk is an absolute fundamental in my opinion in recovery and future protection from narcissistic abuse. It is not always so easy and it takes work and time.

A telling way to tune into your inner self-talk is to try and notice what automatically goes through your mind when you stub your toe, drop your phone or spill something. Is it at all scathing or along the lines of '*oh, I'm so clumsy, what an idiot I am, I always do that, I should be more careful...*' Or is it a kinder, compassionate and patient voice that gently reminds us that accidents happen and there is no need to worry, nothing is broken, that all will be OK? What would the self-talk be if you lost your job or if a partner ended the relationship today? Are you quick to berate yourself or tell yourself '*It's my fault*'? What does your self-talk say about any recent relationship issues?

Negative and destructive self-talk tells us things like:

I should
I can't
I must
I will never be able to
I don't deserve…
Berating statements such as "stupid", "fat", "ugly"
This/I will never change
There's something wrong with me
I'm doomed
It's my fault
I haven't done enough
I'm not good enough
Things will never get any better
It's too late
If anybody else knew they'd think I was mad/bad/stupid

Negative self-talk can be blatant yet it can also be incredibly subtle. It almost always includes a case of the '*shoulds*'. 'Should' is a very loaded and pressurised thing to say. It is fuelled with a sense of obligation and expectation, rather than a kind want or choice. *Should* also strongly relates to, and feeds a sense of shame, guilt and blame. Listen out for the 'should' in your own negative self-talk as this is rarely helpful.

We can learn to counter negative, unhelpful self-talk by first of all tuning in and recognising our automatic internal chatter. As we recognise harsh, destructive, restrictive thinking, we can then start to replace that with self talk that is kinder, friendlier and more supportive.

Kinder, compassionate self talk is more like:

I will try
I'm doing my best

I will see what that's like
I can have a go and see
I can...
I would like...
It's OK to rest
I need...
It would be nice to...
I give myself time to relax or enjoy what I want to
I am fine just the way I am
I am allowed to feel what I feel
I give myself permission
This is how I feel right now... it won't last
I deserve...
It's OK to say 'no'
It's OK / It will be OK / I am OK

Reflection point:

How did your family talk to you and each other when you were growing up? Did you hear them judge others? Were they critical? Would they berate when they or you didn't get things right? Were they gentle and supportive in their words? Were they patient and kind? How did they talk about each other, the neighbours, others? Was it with kindness and compassion? Or bitter, resentful or judgemental? Forgiving or unforgiving? Patient? Tolerant? Understanding?

How do you talk to yourself? Specifically, notice how you talk to yourself when you make a mistake or things are difficult... Is it kind and loving? Supportive? Compassionate? Or harsh, criticising and punitive?

Develop your attention to take notice of your inner self-talk as well as the *tone* of this inner voice.

Notice how you automatically respond to things each day and gently ask yourself how kind and how helpful it is to speak to yourself in this way. Do not beat yourself up about it! This is about recognising, increasing your self-awareness and creating some kind space in order to facilitate gentle, more compassionate, supportive and helpful change.

It can be helpful to consider how you might respond or talk to a dear friend or loved one facing the same predicament. Consider somebody you really care about going through the same thing or feeling the same way. Or even talking to themselves in the same manner. How would you respond to them? What would you say to a best friend or a loved one? How would you support, comfort or reassure them? How would you say it? Is there a difference between how you would talk to a loved one and how you might talk to yourself? If so, why?

20.   The Grief Process

A process of grief following the realisation, change or end of a significant relationship is commonplace. This is also relevant in relation to narcissistic abuse. Kubler-Ross and Kesslers (2005) outline five stages of grief that also capture the process of loss, adaption to change and the ending of relationships.

Denial
Denial is the first stage of grief and loss. The shock of abusive actions can sometimes be so much that we can't compute what has happened. The suddenness of a change in our reality or perspective can be too much that we simply can't quite believe or accept it. So we deny it has happened or is happening. Denial is a stage of processing. However with narcissistic abuse, continuing to deny the extent of the issues is dangerous. That's why earlier chapters in this book included how to connect more with the reality of the situation and address any fantasy thinking. Otherwise denial can cushion the blow of the shock as we begin to process our loss or grief.

Anger
Anger is a perfectly understandable and legitimate feeling to have. As you process your experience you may at times be met

with overwhelming hurt, pain and anger. These are appropriate feelings to have and I would encourage you to allow them to surface. Suppressed anger turns inward and is destructive. Learning ways to express anger can help you to move through it much more quickly. You might find it helpful to pen a letter with all the things you'd want to say or get off your chest. You don't need to send it. You might want to punch a pillow or scream. Identify what or who you are angry about. It may be more than the narcissist. Let your anger out and let it go.

Bargaining

Bargaining is when we try to negotiate our experience in an attempt to ease our suffering. This is the "What if..." stage. Again, much like the initial denial stage, bargaining serves to buffer difficult feelings whilst in time you process further your experience and all the emotions that go with it.

Depression

At points during a grief and loss process, you will likely feel very sad and low. This is not necessarily a mental health issue. Sadness is an appropriate feeling to have in response to difficult change, loss and grief. During this stage you may be tearful, have difficulty sleeping or want to sleep more then usual, experience changes in appetite or lose hope and motivation. It's important to reach out for support and self-care during this tough time.

Acceptance

Reaching acceptance when it comes to narcissistic abuse is a key milestone in your recovery. This is when you feel you can accept what has happened without any need to control or change it. This does not mean you are OK with what has happened or are fine about abuse. It's more about accepting what is and has been in a way you are able to move forward and move on.

The grief process is not always a clear, tidy order. It can feel a bit two steps forward and two steps back. Expect there will be tough days and better days. The main this is to continue to learn and to develop a kinder, more forgiving and compassionate response to yourself and your experience. Try to maintain some focus on your feelings and your self-care needs. The grief process is a process. It will come to an end in time.

21. Trauma & Narcissistic Abuse

Being in a relationship with a narcissist is more often than not traumatising. The abuse, the lies, the denial, gaslighting, the confusion and doubts, the discoveries, realisations, the vitriol, the cheating, stealing and so on... Experiencing trauma in itself can make it difficult to gain or hold a healthier perspective and can be a factor in why people find it difficult to leave an abusive relationship, as is seen in 'trauma bonding'. In this chapter I wish to explain a bit about what trauma is, what causes it, how to recognise it and also some practical tools about how to manage times when you feel triggered in any way.

WHAT IS TRAUMA?

Essentially, trauma describes a psychological or emotional response to any kind of event that has been experienced as significantly distressing or disturbing. Generally speaking, psychological or emotional trauma can arise from *any* experience that threatens our sense of safety or personal security. This can include being involved in or witnessing a road traffic accident, a personal attack, sexual assault, violence or perhaps experiencing a sudden illness, loss or injury. In more extreme cases this also captures being involved in conflict, war or torture (Van Der Kolk, 2014).

When it comes to being in a relationship with a narcissist, trauma can come from virtually any time we have felt unsafe or have experienced a shock to the system. Typically this can include moments of the narcissists sudden 'switch' in mood or behaviour, an angry or aggressive outburst, or the shock of discovering they have lied, stolen or cheated. It can also arise from the complicated confusion of emotional abuse. Complex trauma describes repeated or long term exposure to these kinds of experiences, abuse or neglect. This is usually alongside a lack of support or connection during difficult times too. Trauma often leaves us feeling very isolated and alone.

Trauma explained

Our brains are processing information all the time. We won't necessarily notice, yet information is being automatically processed by parts of our brain all day long. As this information is processed, the events and our experiences from throughout the day are seamlessly processed and filed away, if necessary, into our memory. When we experience a trauma however, or a shock or overwhelm to the system of any kind, then this normal information processing is disrupted. This is because when we experience a shock or trauma our primitive instinct automatically interrupts this as survival takes priority. A trauma will automatically activate a number of powerful physiological responses that are designed to keep us safe and to help us stay alive. Our adrenal glands flood the system with adrenalin and cortisol, creating a strong surge of energy. Our primitive "fight or flight" response is activated. We are instinctively propelled to stay and fight or to run and escape the threat. Other survival responses exist which will be explained further shortly. In the face of a threat, perceived or real, our bodies are completely concerned with survival over anything else in that moment. The surge of neurochemicals and hormones through the system overrides and shuts off the pre-frontal cortex, hippocampus and higher level functioning parts of the brain and instead focuses on bodily survival responses. Basically this instinctive response is saying; *'no time to think or reflect right now, now is simply the time to survive – fight or run!'* Because in the moment of panic or trauma the primary instinct is for survival, our brains are simply unable to process the experience in the way it is usually does with more everyday, non-threatening experiences. At the moment of shock or trauma our physiology is flooded with hormones and neurochemicals and parts of the higher brain are cut-off and shut-down. The information or experience is then not able to be filed away into our memory properly. Instead, fragments of the stressful or traumatic experience are left unprocessed and non-filed, affecting our neural and nervous system (Van Der Kolk, 2014; Ogden, Minton & Pain, 2006).

Specifically, the amygdala is a part of the limbic system in the brain that basically acts as an alarm system. It serves a vital function in that it helps us to sense danger and is alert to any kind of threat. When the amygdala is activated it sends immediate and powerful signals across the brain and body that triggers our core survival instincts – fight, flight or freeze. This reaction overrides any cognitive or logical parts of our brain because faced in the immediate moment of a threat, our primal instinct is to focus solely on surviving. And thats what it does. There is no time for reflection or analysis when we are confronted with significant danger such as a road traffic accident, sexual or physical assault. However, what happens when we have trauma or PTSD is that the amygdala tends to remain on high alert. The amygdala is like a smoke alarm. If we have trauma it becomes very sensitive. The amygdala senses any danger. Just like a smoke alarm, it is also not able to determine if the smoke or threat is just a little bit of burnt toast or if the whole neighbourhood is on fire. It activates the fight-flight-freeze response regardless. The hippocampus usually works to file memories in the brain. In times of high stress or danger, this stops working when we experience a trauma and instead pumps cortisol into our system to support our survival fight or flight response. So because the hippocampus is then unable to process the experience into memory, the event remains unprocessed. This leaves us vulnerable to having any fragment of that memory triggered, and setting off the amygdala key response (Van Der Kolk, 2014).

When the experience is not able to be filed into our memory as usual then that leaves us with a dysregulated nervous system. Fragments of the original memory or trauma remain unprocessed and linger in our neural circuit. When we experience any kind of reminder of the unprocessed memory it can trigger that neural circuit and we then feel as though we are re-experiencing the original trauma. What this means in real terms is that we are left feeling like we are reacting or over-reacting to certain triggers. It is distressing and upsetting, we feel extremely threatened, hyper vigilant or alone. We may find we are a lot more on edge and tearful. It then doesn't take much to make us jumpy, anxious, depressed, numb, nervous, irritable or feeling detached and so on.

As our brains have not been able to process the original traumatic experience, it cannot process and file the experience into memory. With unprocessed experiences, it leaves us vulnerable to having parts of that memory triggered at any time we are reminded of any part of it. It could be a smell, a sound, a vision, a physical sensation, even a thought. Anything can trigger an old traumatic memory and bring all the overwhelming feelings of that time straight back, as if it is happening again in the now. This is essentially post-traumatic stress. Trauma has no sense of time. This in itself can be very distressing and confusing. Parts of our brain may have some sense that we are not in imminent threat in the now, however simultaneously our physiological system will be overwhelmed (Ogden, Minton & Pain, 2006). It will be flooding the system with a panic alert. We may notice that we are strongly reacting to the current situation and be left feeling confused as to why. If you find that your reaction to moments that happen in the now feel much more loaded than perhaps they may warrant then this can sometimes be an indicator that your reaction may in some way be trauma-related.

Trauma can be defined as anything that is too shocking or sudden, out of our control or for whatever reason, too overwhelming for our brains to be able to process in that moment. Unprocessed trauma not only leaves us with symptoms of trauma and PTSD, such as flashbacks and nightmares it can also leave us with maladaptive, unhelpful or destructive ways of thinking, coping or behaving. Sometimes people with unresolved trauma end up using drugs or drinking too much, or engaging in risky sexual behaviours. It also relates to obsessive-compulsive disorders, anxiety disorders, panic attacks, eating disorders and depression. Sometimes trauma can make it feel very difficult to end destructive relationships. Specifically in relation to narcissistic abuse, partners often develop a high level of tolerance for stress and abuse. As the abuse is usually progressive, it can be harder to identify as you can become more and more used to and become increasingly tolerant of it. Feeling like you are somewhat immune to abuse is often due to some adaption to trauma and effectively living in 'survival' mode. This is when you are just about functioning and getting through each day, perhaps sometimes unsure as to even how. Many people living with narcissistic abuse are living in survival mode. Operating in survival mode is in itself a sign of trauma. It can feel a little unreal, numb, like you are disconnected or dissociated.

Narcissistic abuse is a damaging relational trauma. If you suspect you have experienced or are experiencing trauma or symptoms of PTSD, it will be important to seek the right kind of specialist help with this. This can be especially crucial if your trauma, including feelings of fear, guilt or shame, are interfering with your ability to leave, end the relationship or to hold healthy boundaries.

WHAT ARE THE SYMPTOMS OF PTSD & TRAUMA?

* Hyper-vigilant states
* Shock & Disbelief
* Denial
* Confusion
* Anger, Irritability, Mood Swings
* Tearfulness
* Anxiety and Panic
* Feelings of Guilt or Shame
* Depression
* Having a sense of urgency
* Hopelessness
* Suicidal thoughts
* Isolation / Avoidance
* Feeling numb, detached or disconnected
* Difficulty sleeping
* Waking up during the night or early in the morning with anxiety, panic, flashbacks or nightmares.
* Intrusive thoughts or images
* Obsessions / Obsessiveness
* Constantly feeling on edge or jumpy
* Difficulties with boundaries or saying 'no'
* Difficulty leaving or ending a toxic abusive relationship
* Feeling 'stuck'
* Physical sensations; e.g.. nausea, sickness, palpitations, dizziness, trembling.

STRESS OR TRAUMA REACTIONS

We all have an instinctive, innate and automatic responses to stress or trauma. Fight or flight is most commonly discussed and understood however, there are other reactions which can be experienced in response to the various aspects of narcissistic abuse. They are outlined below:

Fight

Fight captures our innate instinct to fight back, to lash out and stay and protect ourselves. This can include becoming very angry, aggressive and physically attacking in defence. Outward anger reflects a way of being that is very challenging, provocative, intrusive and threatening to others. People who tend to react in a fight response can be mistrustful or paranoid. They may also reject support, believing they must go it alone and can't trust or rely on anybody else. There is little emotional tolerance. Inward and internalised anger can become dangerous and can relate to violent acts towards yourself, such as self-harm or suicidal thoughts.

Flight

Flight describes the instinctive urge to run and seek to escape from the situation. It is a strong primitive survival instinct that automatically floods the system with hormones in order to help you mobilise, run and escape. Through this kind of anxiety one may attempt to avoid or distance themselves from triggering external situations or relationships. There may be an attempt to avoid any internal conflict or emotional experience, for example, using drink, drugs or food in order to change or escape from difficult feelings.

Freeze

Another primitive survival instinct that leaves you feeling quite immobilised. In a freeze response, you feel fearful and highly anxious, to the point where you feel unable to action. Instead, you feel like you cannot move or speak and may feel like you wish to hide or disappear. In a freeze response you may also experience nightmares, flashbacks and intrusive thoughts or images.

Flop

A common response in particular relation to narcissistic abuse is one of submission. With a 'flop' reaction we feel as though we have given up. We shut down and barely respond any longer in an instinctive bid for survival. This can feel somewhat numb. You may feel tired, unmotivated, fatigued and perhaps even experience psychosomatic symptoms. With this reaction we are submissive and don't want to cause any bother, we fear upsetting or displeasing others. We say "whatever" and give up any fight. We may also experience guilt and shame.

(be)Friend

This reaction is a complicated one in cases of abuse and really encapsulates the survival instinct of staying close to a 'caregiver'. In this reaction, at times of stress or trauma we become highly reliant on others to provide us with support and comfort. We seek to attach. This neediness and at times, desperation can also become skewed. People may tend to believe they are completely helpless and need another to support, rescue and save them. They become attached and may even manipulate in order to get their needs met, appearing sweet, childlike and helpless. Those in this style of response need to be liked and can fear abandonment.

MODULATION – WINDOW OF TOLERANCE

The 'Window of Tolerance' (WOT) is a modulation model of the nervous system originally coined by Dr. Dan Siegel (1999) – a clinical professor of psychiatry and trauma specialist. It describes our brain/body reactions at times of stress or trauma. The model describes that we have an ideal range of optimal arousal within the nervous system, referred to as the 'window of tolerance'. Within this range there is room for slight ups and downs and ebbs and flows of variation depending on activities or stress levels, although usually we are largely able to stay within this range and things feel OK. Our window of tolerance is our range in which we are comfortable, able to function at our best and can make decisions from.

At times of extreme stress, arousal or trauma, including when any unprocessed trauma is re-triggered, just as it with narcissistic abuse, our nervous system response quickly shifts to outside of our window of tolerance. It either shoots to above and beyond the window of tolerance in *hyperarousal* or drops way below and bottoms out of the WOT into *hypoarousal*. These responses are also connected to our primitive survival instinct (Ogden, Minton & Pain, 2006; Siegel, 1999).

Hyperarousal is a state characterised by feelings of heightened panic and anxiety, fear and hypervigilance. If we are hyperaroused we are very much on edge, highly stressed, nervous, agitated, perhaps even angry or irritable. Our nervous system is flooded and overwhelmed. We find it difficult to relax, we feel emotional, restless and experience difficulties with eating or sleeping. Hyperarousal is very much an 'on high alert' system activation.

Hypoarousal is very much the opposite. This bottoming-out describes dropping below the Window of Tolerance and is a response when our system is overwhelmed to the point that it goes into 'shut-down and switch-off' mode. In this state we feel numb, detached, disconnected, dissociated, flat, depressed and/ or fatigued. We may feel like we have nothing in us and have nothing to give and simply want to take to bed.

Stress and unprocessed trauma, both of which go hand in hand with narcissistic abuse, can unsettle and disrupt the nervous system. This means that we can find that we rapidly shift into being either above or below our window of tolerance. Either side is distressing and detrimental to our mental health and wellbeing. Experiences of and living with narcissistic abuse are enough to shift us outside of our window of tolerance and feel stuck in either hyper or hyper-arousal, perhaps even oscillating between the too. This can be at specific moments or in long-term abuse can become a more adapted way of being. Additionally, when under significant or ongoing stress our optimal window of tolerance range shrinks and effectively becomes very narrow. With that being very narrow, it doesn't then take much too much more stress or agitation to push us into a hyper or hypo arousal state.

As you familiarise yourself with this model, as well as with the specific stress/trauma reactions above, you may find that you recognise this more in yourself as it happens. Recognising aspects of this as it happens can be very helpful in helping reduce the level of physiological arousal. The moment we become consciously and mindfully aware of what is going on, we immediately bring space to it – rather than feeling completely overwhelmed or consumed. We can observe what is happening in a mindful, objective and compassionate way, rather than reacting to it or letting whatever is happening completely overwhelm us or pull us away with it. When old trauma is triggered it can feel a bit like getting sucked into a vortex. The following techniques can help you to resist getting sucked into it. So it can be useful to help ease and manage times when you may feel either too hyper or hypo aroused by using a number of different techniques. The most suitable tools depend on whether you are above or below your window of tolerance. The best thing to do is to work to identify what you recognise in your own reactions and see which techniques work best for you.

Techniques to help reduce and calm hyper-arousal

* Mindful attention and awareness. This involves *just noticing* what is happening within you in the present moment. Notice any thoughts, feelings or any physical sensations. Mindful attention means with no desire to change, you just observe. You can even make a mental note or name the things you notice.

* Increase your awareness of your physical and physiological states. Notice physical sensations or feelings starting from top to bottom. Head, jaw, chest, breath, neck and shoulders, tummy, arms and legs... just notice what the sensations are. For example, tension, tingling, energy, numbness, coldness, heat and so on.

* Get present. Trauma has no sense of time so when it is triggered, parts of us do not recognise that we are in a different situation to the original trauma. Take a look around, ground yourself in the present moment. Remind yourself that you can be and are OK right now.

* Use your senses to ground and centre yourself.

* Practice self-soothing. As you bring awareness to the different sensations you notice in the body, then use the focus to breathe into any areas of unease and gently let go and release any contractions or tension. Reassure and tell yourself you are OK.

* Slow deep breathing – for as long as is necessary to calm the hyperarousal. Deep yogic breaths can help calm the nervous system with a few minutes. Specifically, exhaling for twice as long as you inhale can help calm, reduce tension and stress. Using this breathing technique along with focusing on specific parts of the body where you feel any reaction can be especially helpful. You can use control of the breath in this way to importantly help send a message from the body back to the brains alarm system that says *"I am OK, I am safe"*.

* Go for a walk.
* Exercise. Slow rhythmic movement can help. This could be walking, a light jog, yoga, swimming or tai chi.
* Mindfulness meditation. Mindfulness of breath and can help calm hyperarousal.
* Make a warm relaxing drink. A calming herbal tea such as chamomile can help.
* Distract your attention by doing something completely different – preparing some food, cleaning or sorting.
* Phone a friend or talk to somebody that may help ease your feelings.
* Listen to some calming or soothing music.
* Smell some soothing or calming scents, like lavender.
* Cuddle. A person or pet.

*On occasions, sometimes you may find a hyper-aroused state is not helped by trying to soothe and calm yourself via the kinds of techniques outlined above. Sometimes there is more of an excess charge of energy in the system that is actually best shifted and moved up and out. This can often be more helpful if you identify you have more of a freeze response. If this is the case you may also like to try:

* Get very intensely physically active. Go for a run. Stomp your feet on the ground. Squats. Press ups or push ups until you feel the energy discharges.
* Scream.
* Punch a cushion.
* Throw a ball.

Some ideas for increasing arousal from hypo-arousal include

* The same mindfulness and body-awareness techniques as described above.

* Getting up to move and activate the body. Walk, stretch, jump, dance, swim – tap, squeeze or massage parts of the body. Push-Ups or squats – anything to get the body moving and energised
* Anything to activate and stimulate the senses.
* Go outside and breath in the fresh air. Take deep, energising breaths.
* Smell a strong (non-triggering) scent, such as coffee or essential oils.
* Walk bare foot on grass.
* Eat strong tasting or crunchy food. Awaken the taste buds and senses.
* Touch and explore textures.
* Play some uplifting music.
* Get out in the daylight.

One more thing to know is that when any of our unprocessed trauma is triggered at all, whether you recognise a hyper or hypo-arousal response, our brains response in that present moment does not identify any timeframe. Unprocessed trauma is timeless. When we are triggered, old experiences and parts of the original traumatic memory come flooding back and feel like the original trauma is happening all over again in that moment. By using mindful awareness, awareness of the physical body and breath, as well as the other techniques outlined above you can help to calm this response and help soothe yourself. It may also be particularly helpful to try in whichever way you to remind yourself of the present moment. Try to ground or centre yourself in *'right here, right now'*, so that you can try to support conscious feedback to the brain via the senses that you are perhaps not in the level of danger you may have been at the time of the original trauma. The physiology won't necessarily recognise that. But through conscious awareness we can support that feedback and help to settle ourselves (Ogden, Minton & Pain, 2006). This could include slowly orientating yourself to the current environment, looking all around you and identifying objects or things you can see. Label them in your mind or out loud. It may help to physically touch things around you, the chair, the wall, the floor. Use these sturdy and stable items to remind yourself that you are safe now, that you can be safe now. Of course, developing self-compassion is crucial for these times too. Hopefully, you have already started to work on the topics discussed in earlier chapters and find a deepening sense of inner gentleness, kindness and support. The magic is when that practice is utilised at more distressing times. When anxiety or old traumas are triggered, there is often an associated punitive self-talk that tells us things are catastrophic, that things will never change or improve and that we are doomed. A voice of self-compassion reminds us very calmly things like; *I am OK, this will pass, this is just old stuff, I am safe now, things will be fine, this won't last* and so on.

Try to find which particular techniques you like or work best for you. The more you practice these the easier you will find it to use when you need them. Try not to just wait until you are triggered before you attempt to use these tools. The more you practice, the more you can get to grips with what helps. Regular practice can also help calm and settle disruptions in the nervous system. Over time, this can help reduce the level of reaction you may experience. Body awareness, mindfulness practices, breath work and yoga are all helpful practices. I am a huge advocate for the power of a regular mindful yoga asana and breath practice to help calm the nervous system and to help all of what is discussed here feel more manageable. There are also certain psychotherapies that specifically help to process unprocessed trauma. If you recognise that you have specific triggers or suspect you have trauma I cannot recommend enough that you seek to find good individual trauma therapy. A good trauma therapist will help you to process any unresolved traumatic experiences in a way that is gentle, safe and effective. As you process any unprocessed trauma, you ease any of the associated symptoms or triggers that go alongside that. It can offer great relief and support a restoration of peace, contentment, sense of safety, restoration of boundaries and more. Some recommended trauma therapy approaches are outlined in the next section.

THERAPY FOR TRAUMA AND PTSD

I think that if relevant, it is a good idea to seek a specialist trauma therapist to help with any specific traumatic or troubling aspects of your experience of narcissistic abuse. Not everybody needs this, but I personally believe that if you feel you are experiencing any ongoing significant concerns, anxieties or find yourself triggered by memories or even find it hard to let go and move on, then specialist trauma therapies can help. I mention specific trauma therapies too because if you work with a trauma therapist who can help you to identify your key traumas then these are things that can be worked through and processed relatively quickly and safely, in a way that can bring you relief. I am aware of certain systems that suggest you undertake trauma recovery or healing on your own. If that is what you seek to do then I completely respect that decision – after all I think it is important to develop a sense and trust into your own instinct about what is right for you. However, for me, I personally would not recommend attempting it alone. There are a number of reasons why I share that. Firstly, when old trauma is triggered it can very much feel like you are being sucked into a vortex of old memories, feelings or sensations. Sometimes they can be so powerful and strong that it is very difficult, if not impossible, to independently help yourself to return from that and ground or centre yourself. It will happen in time, but in some instances it can take days, if not weeks or longer. A trained trauma therapist will be watching that you do not reach the limit of feeling so triggered as you do this work.

They will support you to a place where your nervous system and memory is activated just enough in order for you to process the trauma, but without being overwhelmed. By going it alone you can run the risk of triggering an emotional overwhelm or even re-traumatisation. Another reason why I would encourage working with a therapist is because of the very nature of the trauma related to narcissistic abuse. It is relational trauma. In other words it is a trauma or betrayal between one person and another. A common response in people who have experienced narcissistic abuse, particularly if their family life or childhood was unsupportive, is a tendency to then be super self-reliant. I experienced this myself, but recognised that in part, is part of an issue. By working with a therapist you can overcome and work through numerous aspects of relational trauma by directly experiencing all the aspects of a therapeutic relationship. Therapy offers a chance to experience a particular kind of relationship, to talk through issues, to communicate and to develop trust. Working closely with a therapist in this way can in itself be a crucial part of healing from trauma and abuse. I personally recommend the following therapy approaches for narcissistic abuse based on my personal experience as well as what I use in my own practice.

EMDR Therapy

Eye Movement Desensitisation & Reprocessing (EMDR) Therapy is a powerful psychotherapeutic technique that aids the processing of trauma and complex grief, reducing symptoms of PTSD. EMDR therapy, by using bilateral stimulation (which basically means left and right brain activity) whilst focusing on a memory or experience, helps the brain to gently process any unprocessed trauma. Generally speaking, we can tell if we have unprocessed memories that may be helped by EMDR if we find we get upset, tearful or troubled at all when bring it to mind or talk about it. Feeling particularly sensitive about things, situations or reacting in a way that may be considered above and beyond what the current situation warrants could be signs of unprocessed trauma. EMDR won't erase memories, however it can help to ease the associated pain so that they are much less upsetting. In recovery from narcissistic abuse I personally aim to help clients be able to talk about or recall their past toxic relationships if they so wish without it feeling at all emotive. Recollecting the past in a neutral way and in a way where the past feels like it is where it belongs, ie. in the past, is a good indicator that the experience has been processed and of recovery. I really like to use EMDR in my clinical practise because people tend to like it and find it an effective, gentle and relatively fast way to process trauma and move people forward in recovery from narcissistic abuse. You can find EMDR therapists via directories or search engines in your region. Please check out the EMDR association in your area for more information.

Sensorimotor Psychotherapy

Sensorimotor psychotherapy is a body-based approach founded by Pat Ogden in the early 80's. From her work as a yoga and dance teacher she became more interested in psychology and mind/body disconnect whilst working in a psychiatric hospital in the 70's. It was from here that she began to recognise what we now understand as PTSD as held in the mind and body. In PTSD, various reminders of past traumatic experiences trigger painful and distressing memories. Unprocessed trauma in itself leaves us with some disconnect between mind and body. Ogden developed specific body based interventions and methods – further developed and including the Hakomi method as pioneered by Ron Kurtz – in order to establish a mind-body reconnection and integration. By doing so, symptoms of trauma, stress reactions and anxiety can be relieved. Sensorimotor psychotherapy draws from a number of theoretical approaches including from the field of neuroscience, analytical and mindfulness therapies.

Somatic Experiencing

Somatic experiencing is another form of therapy that focuses on bodily sensations as a way of relieving symptoms of trauma and PTSD. Developed by Peter Levine, this approach involved mindful tracking of body sensations and inner experience. This approach also helps to calm the nervous system and to support clients to find ways in which to return to a more regulated state. Again, both of these bottom-up body-based therapeutic approaches are gentle, supportive and aid recovery from abuse and trauma.

Somatic Psychology and psychotherapy approaches such as Sensorimotor Psychotherapy and Somatic Experiencing as well as Eye Movement Desensitisation and Reprocessing (EMDR) are all very helpful in bringing together and restoring a mindful and conscious mind-body connection. They are very effective for helping to process trauma. These types of therapies importantly help to support the gentle reconnection of any disconnected parts, due to trauma or painful or difficult memories, feelings or experiences, including narcissistic abuse. This supports the development and re-establishment of communication and trust between our minds and our bodies, our inner sense or knowing.

Importantly, these approaches do not require you to talk about or go into all the ins and outs of any traumatic memories and so it's less likely to be re-traumatising. Instead these therapies help to gently and swiftly support the processing of any unprocessed material and subsequently bring about a huge sense of relief from any troubling symptoms. Many people report feeling much better after just a handful of sessions of the right kinds of trauma therapy. The key is searching to find the right kind of trauma therapy with the right therapist for you. Trauma therapy should always be a supportive and gentle process. As far as I'm concerned, if you have trauma, then you've already been through enough – any input from this point should be gentle, supportive and compassionate.

22. Gratitude and Acknowledgement

I would like to suggest you try out the following powerful daily practice at this stage too. This does not only help support a more compassionate inner self-talk for yourself, but it can also shift your perspective in a similar way. This can therefore importantly support your ongoing growth and recovery from narcissistic abuse. The power of acknowledgement and gratitude is not to be underestimated in my opinion. It can offer an incredibly powerful psychological shift and be an important fundamental practice in positive mental wellbeing. I can appreciate gratitude may be a strange concept to consider at this time. However, a sense of gratitude can powerfully shift your perspective and positively change your experience, especially following difficult times.

Listing things you are grateful for at the end of each day is a consistent effort to bring about a helpful and positive shift in perspective. This may, or may not seem like an impossible task to start with, yet, if you can list just one or two things you genuinely feel grateful for each day, then that is a great start. In time you will find you can add more and more to your daily gratitude list.

Try writing a gratitude list each evening. List whatever it is you feel grateful for, for that day, no matter how big or small you may think it is! Aim for 10, or feel free to write as many things as you like.

Some examples of items for a gratitude list to help get started with may include:

I'm grateful to have a roof over my head tonight.
I'm grateful I have eaten well today.
I'm grateful to be out of a toxic situation.
I'm grateful for my children/friends/family.
I'm grateful for the support and understanding of my friend/s.
I'm grateful for all I am learning.
I'm grateful I can read.
I'm grateful I have my dog.
I'm grateful I am learning about healthy relationships.
I'm grateful I can make positive choices for myself now.
I'm grateful I have my job.
I'm grateful for my health.
I'm grateful for a nice walk in nature today.
I am grateful for coffee!
I am grateful for experiencing moments of peace now.
I am grateful I am learning how to look after myself.
I'm grateful for the stranger who smiled at me today.
I'm grateful for my higher power.
I'm grateful for the insights and awareness I'm gaining.
I'm grateful for the weather.
I'm grateful I was able to check in on my neighbour today.
I'm grateful I'm not a narcissist.
I'm grateful for my freedom.
I'm grateful to be alive.

ACKNOWLEDGEMENT

Another thing you might also like to add to your daily evening list is acknowledging whatever it is you feel you did well today. Or that you feel good for doing today. Be specific. Again, no matter how big or small it may seem. This is also a powerful tool in building a self-esteem, kinder self-talk and a healthier perspective of yourself.

Examples of this can include:

I got up today!
I was productive. I got some things done today.
I exercised.
I ate well today – I made healthy food choices.
I was there for my friend today, as best as I could be, who is having a difficult time. I'm a good friend.
I did well at work today, speaking in a meeting even though I was nervous.
I rested when I needed to.
I cleaned.
I helped my elderly neighbour with her shopping today.
I was kind.
I took the dog for a walk.
I called my mother and managed to speak to her without getting angry or upset.
I did yoga.
I paid a bill.
I made an important decision.
and so on...

This is your list, for you. So add absolutely whatever you want to add to it. No judgements.

> *Reflection point:*
>
> * What do I feel grateful for today?
> * What can I be grateful for out of my experiences?
> * What do I acknowledge in myself today?

As this is for you and about kindness, compassion, gratitude and self-care you may like to treat yourself to a lovely new notebook and pen for this purpose. Find whatever you would like to write in and make this a few minutes of time for you to reflect and recognise anything and everything you feel grateful for, each day. I do believe there is a power in writing in black and white and in paper and pen, rather than in digital format. It may also be interesting to look back in time at earlier lists. The main thing is to keep with it. Take some time for this every evening. Ideally in the evening so you can reflect back on your day. Make it part of your daily routine, just like you would getting washed or brushing your teeth and getting ready for bed. Some days may feel easier than others. Some days you might struggle to come up with a few things, others days it may be more free-flowing. The main thing is start. Start today. And then keep with it, on a daily basis and see what happens from there... Start today. Practice this each and every day and then see what changes you notice in a few weeks time.

23.   Advice for Friends & Family...

Watching a loved one suffer at the hands of any kind of abuse is obviously painful. Often friends, family or colleagues of somebody in an abusive relationship are left confused, struggling to understand why he/she simply cannot see how awful they are being treated and why they cannot simply leave. Advice and pleas fall on seemingly deaf ears. It is understandably very upsetting to see a loved one struggle, and frustrations and feelings can get in the way of knowing what to do. Many times I have heard people describe that they feel helpless and unable or unwilling to get involved so I wanted to include some suggestions and pointers as to how we might best spot and respond to others with suspected narcissistic abuse.

One of the first things to note is that abuse of any kind is absolutely unacceptable, and under the remit of domestic violence, is also against the law. Physical abuse is the most obvious kind of abuse to spot. It is a criminal offence and it's important that if you suspect physical violence of any kind that you report this to the police. This can even be done anonymously if you have any concerns. Unfortunately, most narcissists are usually smarter than to leave any noticeable marks for others to see. Narcissistic abuse is otherwise known as 'invisible abuse' because it is usually much more emotionally, psychologically, controlling and manipulative. Many ex-victims of narcissistic abuse report that they wish there had been an episode of physical violence as it would have made it easier to recognise this as abuse. I have also heard many clients remark such things along the lines of "oh, but he/she never hit me..." as if that is the marker for abuse. It's not. UK government guidance has recently been updated to include psychological, emotional and financial controlling and threatening behaviours as definitions of abuse.

A narcissist will leave a partner / colleague / family member with a considerable sense of low self-esteem, self-worth and self doubt. Being trapped in a narcissistic relationship leaves a person feeling like *'it's me'*, *'it's my fault'*. Those on the outside can see more clearly that most certainly is not. So it can be helpful to remind your loved one that it is NOT their fault.

Abusive behaviour is <u>never</u> anybody else's fault or responsibility – other than the abusers.

We are all responsible for our own actions. Narcissists are responsible for their own actions (they just won't accept that... and that by the way, is *also* their responsibility. Not yours.

Reality and a grounded perspective will become quite distorted for those involved with a narcissist. They will be accustomed to being told in a variety of ways, that essentially they are wrong and they are the problem. eg. *"If you weren't so possessive then I wouldn't need to cheat"*.

It can be helpful to remind our friend or loved one that it is <u>not</u> them – and that the narcissist is being unfair and abusive.

Try to support your loved one to see their own positive qualities – to help them build strong and healthy self-esteem.

It can also be helpful to offer a comparison to help give some perspective on other, healthier relationships. e.g. "If I told my partner I had got a promotion, they would be genuinely happy for me and supportive of that... not make out I am being bigheaded or arrogant for doing well or react negatively in any other way.

Remind and reassure them what you believe is OK and not OK behaviour or comments in a relationship / work environment or whatever the situation.

Narcissists will consciously or otherwise want to isolate their partner. We are much more vulnerable on our own and without social support. Please look out for this as a sign. Who is the friend or colleague that misses social functions? Or has to leave early? Has contact from their partner all night long anxiously checking where they are and with who? Are they being checked up on, or punished in any way for having some time out?

A dangerous position for somebody being isolated is when friends or family stop being in touch. One thing you can do is check-in and encourage them to be in touch and to reach out. Gently encourage them to talk about how *they* are, how *they* are feeling and what's going on for *them* – not their partner.

A skilled narcissist will likely already have planted the seed that *'nobody will believe [you] if you tell anyone anyway'*. If somebody is telling you about a partners abusive actions, believe them.

Be direct in making it clear that the narcissists behaviours or words are not OK / abusive / inappropriate / damaging / hurtful / bullish / intimidating, etc.

Name what you see or hear. You will be in a better position to do so than anybody caught up in this kind of relationship or dynamic.

Being in a relationship with a narcissist can leave anybody feeling like they are going mad. Offer reassurance that they are not losing their mind – but rather this is what this kind of abuse *feels* like.

Assure them that you and others are there for them.

Offer an exit plan, somewhere they can go to or can get in touch anytime if or when they need it. Perhaps even store an emergency bag of items they can leave if they ever need a quick get out.

Don't judge.

Please try to be patient. It is understandably very frustrating to watch the damage from the sidelines, however it takes people different times and certain experiences to realise and see whats happening.

If you become very concerned for welfare or safety or if there are any child safety concerns at all then please contact local services and trained professionals so that they can intervene.

24.

Moving on...

I saw a hand-written sign on the London underground recently that I thought really captures recovery from narcissistic abuse. It was a thought for the day and read:

> **Don't blame a clown for acting like a clown,
> ask yourself why you keep going to the circus**

Narcissists are mentally unwell. Don't take this personally. It is not your fault and most importantly it is not your responsibility to try to make it all better. You are not their shrink. There is no simple cure for narcissism. There is however recovery from narcissistic abuse, echoes and codependency. Your recovery and growth is your responsibility.

I whole-heartedly hope that you have found at least something in what you've read here helpful for your journey. Narcissistic abuse is an awful thing to experience and one that really tests and rattles the sanity of the strongest. When I experienced this myself I was left feeling traumatised. I'd quite literally felt like I'd been pulled into a whirlwind tornado for a period of time and was then thrown out the other side of it. I was all over the place and didn't know what was what. For a short while I could barely eat or sleep and I had a period of time where I was locked onto absolutely needing to understand and make sense of all the madness. I needed to know why he had done what he had done and I wanted to make him see the upset he had caused and to be accountable. One of the most difficult things I recognised I needed to accept and reconcile with was that I did not have answers, and quite probably never would. He was a highly manipulative and convincing compulsive liar. I had to come to accept that I would never get any truth. It was an impossible expectation. It was futile. He was incapable of taking responsibility for himself. It would always be 'my stuff'. As part of my process of recovery I had to let go of *my* need to have him know or think otherwise. I had to let go of my control issues that were causing me distress by feeling the need to put him right and to justify or explain myself or to make him see or behave in any other way than he chooses. He can think whatever he wants to. That is his choice. I no longer need to concern myself with his or anybody else business – and what a relief that is!

A reaction to trauma can be obsession and I had to unhook myself away from thinking so much about him and the relationship. I was trying to make sense but that in itself was like being stuck on a maddening loop. I used mindfulness and yoga practice to help with this and used the techniques I've outlined in this book to help slowly but surely return the focus back to myself. So then I was left with me and my part and I knew that was where the work is. When we stop focusing on others and return our attentions to ourselves we are faced with all parts of ourselves including looking at fears, anxieties, insecurities and old traumas. There were some hard truths in there about my own issues, aspects of my own narcissism and needs to control. More layers were revealed as I worked on myself. It ultimately became a journey of deep self-exploration and recovery. It is one I am infinitely grateful for. I do believe on some level that things happen for a reason and that it's helpful to view challenges as an opportunity to learn and grow from. I can certainly say that following my experience of narcissistic abuse. I am grateful that it was bad enough to propel me into really doing something about it and doing whatever work I needed to do to never go through something like that ever again. I watched friends over the years repeat the same patterns in toxic relationships and go through hell each time and I remember thinking there is absolutely no way I could go through that again – never again. I am infinitely grateful that my experience has also hugely informed my work and it's a dream come true to share some of this experience and knowledge in the hope that it can help others. I think narcissistic abuse is something that you can only really truly understand once you've been through it first-hand. It's a different kind of magic. One that is traumatising in so many ways. My journey has been a process where at times, especially in the beginning, I have felt completely stripped down. I think I actually needed to be in order to build up again – this time with stronger and firmer foundations than ever before. I've really learnt a lot about self-esteem, compassion, boundaries and communication and it's all been for the benefit of life and relationships since then.

I believe a helpful first step, as I've outlined at the beginning of this book, is to really research and understand narcissism and narcissistic abuse. This is in order to support our minds natural need to make sense of our experience. It supports our processing. Then it's essential to find ways to detach from the toxicity and shift your focus back to yourself in a gentle and compassionate way. Then the real work begins. To reiterate a few key points for recovery:

Focus on you
Recovering from an abusive relationship presents you with a real opportunity for positive growth and change. I absolutely believe that you can work to break any destructive relationships patterns, by working on yourself – it's an inside job. This includes focusing

on you and your own actions, issues, your own interests, self-care needs, esteem and allowing your emotional experience. You can't change the narcissist and never will. But YOU can change and grow. And you will be the first to benefit from that too.

Allow yourself to feel
The rollercoaster ride of being with a narcissist leaves a whole range of feelings – some even mixed. You may grieve the relationship. It is an ending and a loss. Allow yourself to grieve. Allow yourself to feel whatever feelings come up. Respond to all of those feeling with gentleness, kindness, forgiveness and compassion.

Use emotional regulation and self-soothe techniques
Using these practical strategies can help you manage the narcissist as well as support your recovery process. They are fundamental to self-care and mental and emotional wellbeing.

Let go of trying to change or control the narcissist
You are a fellow human. You do not have the power to change or control anybody. More to the point, why would you want to? Trying to control or change a narcissist or holding onto a fantasy and hope that they will change is a sure fire way to maintain the madness of narcissistic abuse. A need to control others reflects as much about yourself. You can explore and work through whatever fuels your need to control or change others by returning your focus to yourself.

Take responsibility
One of the most empowering things you can do is to take full responsibility for yourself. Let go of the hope or desire that anybody else will rescue, fix or take responsibility for you. You are responsible for where you place your attention and efforts. You are responsible for your choices. You are responsible for your

life. Embrace and enjoy this opportunity for growth. You take charge when you take full responsibility for yourself. By doing this you can also let go of being over-responsible. Let go of what is not yours or your responsibility.

Let go of any old, unhelpful or inaccurate beliefs

By this I mean letting go of the guilt, blame, fear or sense of responsibility you have for the narcissist. In healthy relationships we allow others take responsibility for themselves. It is in their best interest to learn to become a fully self-responsible adult. At the same time, you can focus on yourself and your choices and let go of and over-responsibility, guilt or fears. Relationships are much healthier and nurturing this way. Let go of any old, unhelpful or inaccurate beliefs you may have about yourself too.

Keep it real

It's so important in recovery to move away from fantasy thinking and get grounded in reality. Feel your feet on the ground and look at what is happening in the present, rather than believing what the narcissist says or getting pulled into any hopes and fantasies about how things might be. Do not believe the promises. Let go of the hope and fantasy that one day things will be miraculously different – that one day the narcissist might change. You are responsible for getting a more accurate, realistic perspective or the situation. Keep it simple and keep it real.

Boundaries, boundaries, boundaries

Whether you are trying to cope within a relationship or manage the end of one, remember boundaries, boundaries, boundaries. Boundaries mean you stay on your side of the street and focus more on what you are doing. Holding boundaries with a narcissist is powerful and key to regaining a sense of control, power and not to mention sanity. Much like a strong tree with solid firm roots deeply grounded, with boundaries we become much less affected or even interested in what the other person is doing, saying or threatening. Healthy boundaries really are the basis for healthy relationships.

Find your tribe

One of the blessings I think that comes from experiencing narcissistic abuse is the potential reshaping of all relationships. As part of the process of recovery, you can really learn about your values and about what is important to you in your life. This includes the kind of people you want in your life and the kind of person you want to be. Finding your community and thriving amongst friends, family or your social support network is so important in so many ways. Support and connection are crucial for our wellbeing. It hasn't got to be a huge team, just a few good friends and people who have your best interests at heart and vice versa in itself can be incredibly healing. Joining a support group or fellowship may help.

As I've mentioned, I do believe that you can absolutely recover and heal from narcissistic abuse and that in time, it can even be an experience to be deeply grateful for. Be clear and committed to yourself. Hone the relationship you have within yourself – that can be the greatest gift you ever give yourself. You can find ways to leave the past exactly where it belongs, in the past; and instead move on and move forward with your life. I wish you all the very best with your recovery and your journey.

Epilogue
The Scorpion and the Frog

There is an old fable about a scorpion and a frog. The scorpion asks the frog to carry it across the river. The frog initially hesitates, his gut instinct senses something is wrong. There is good reason to be cautious. He knows that scorpions sting and he is afraid of getting stung. The scorpion though tells the frog that he won't sting him. The scorpion points out that if it did, they would end up both drowning in the river and there wouldn't be any point in that! The frog thought about it and being the kind of frog that likes to help out agrees to carry the scorpion across the river. Midway across the river, the scorpion stings the frog, they are both immediately doomed. Now, in the middle of deep water, they will both drown. The frog is shocked and stunned by the sting, it leaves him feeling numb and he has difficulty breathing. The frog confused, shaken and upset asks the scorpion why he stung him. The scorpion replied quite simply and matter of factly. "I'm a scorpion... Scorpions sting". It is the nature of a scorpion to sting. We all know that. The frog knew that. However he decided to go against what he knew and his gut instinct and instead went with what the scorpion had told him. The frog put its own life in danger because of his desire to appease and help, he wanted to believe the scorpion. How can the frog expect anything else? The scorpion did what scorpions do.

References & Further Reading

3. What is Narcissism?

American Psychiatric Association. (2013). *Diagnostic and statistical manual of mental disorders* (5th ed.). Arlington, VA: American Psychiatric Publishing.

Gerhardt, S (2004). Why Love Matters: How affection shapes a baby's brain. England: Routledge

Groopman, Leonard C. M.D. & Cooper, Arnold M. M.D. (2006). "Narcissistic Personality Disorder". *Personality Disorders – Narcissistic Personality Disorder*. Armenian Medical Network.

Paris, J. (2014). Modernity and narcissistic personality disorder. *Personality Disorders: Theory, Research & Treatment.* 5.(2). 220-226.

Piaget, J. (1954). *Construction of reality in the child.* (M, Cook, Trans.). New York: Basic Books

Piaget, J. (1977). The Essential Piaget. Gruber, HE; Voneche, JJ. eds. New York: Basic Books

Torgersep, S., Lygren, S., Oien, P.A., Skre, I., Onstad, S., Edvardsen, J., Tambs, K. & Kringlen, E. (2000). A twin study of personality disorders. *Comprehensive Psychiatry.* 41(6). 416-425

Walsh, W. (2014). *Nutrient Power: Heal your biochemistry and heal your brain*. New York: Skyhorse Publishing.

5. Relational Dynamics – The Drama Triangle

MD. Stephen Karpman Drama Triangle website – www.karpmandramatriangle.com

Karpman, S. (2014). *A Game Free Life – The definitive book on the Drama Triangle and Compassion Triangle by the originator and author*. San Francisco: Drama Triangle Publications.

14. Foundations for Recovery – Emotional Regulation

Baer, R. A. (2003). Mindfulness training as a clinical intervention: A conceptual and empirical review. Clinical Psychology: Science and Practice. 10. 125-143.

Chiesa, A & Serretti, A. (2014) Are Mindfulness-Based Interventions Effective for Substance Use Disorders? A Systematic Review of the Evidence, Substance Use & Misuse, 49:5, 492-512.

Kabat-Zinn, J. (2013). *Full Catastrophe Living: Using the Wisdom of Your Body and Mind to Face Stress, Pain, and Illness*. New York: Bantam Dell.

Hofmann, S. G., Sawyer, A. T., Witt, A. A. & Oh, D. (2010). The effect of Mindfulness-Based Therapy on Anxiety and Depression: A Meta-Analytic Review. *Journal of Consulting & Clinical Psychology*. Vol. 78(2); 169-183

The Dialectical Behaviour Therapy Skills Workbook – Practical DBT exercises for Learning Mindfulness, Interpersonal Effectiveness, Emotion Regulation and Distress Tolerance. by Matthew McKay, Jeffrey Wood & Jeffrey Brantley

15. How to Change how you Feel by Changing what you Think

CBT for Dummies *by Rhena Branch & Rob Wilson*

Overcoming Low Self-Esteem: A self help guide using Cognitive Behavioural Techniques *by Melanie Fennell*
Mind over Mood *by Christine Padesky*

20. The Grief Process

Kubler-Ross, E. & Kessler, D. (2005). On Grief & Grieving: Finding the Meaning of Grief Through the Five Stages of Loss. London: Simon & Schuster

21. Trauma & Narcissistic Abuse

Ogden, P., Minton, K., & Pain, C. (2006). Trauma and the body: A sensorimotor approach to psychotherapy. New York: W.W. Norton.

Siegel, D.J. (1999). The developing mind: How relationships and the brain interact to shape who we are. New York; Guilford Press.

Van Der Kolk, B. (2014). The Body Keeps the Score: Brain, Mind, and Body in the Healing of Trauma. New York: Penguin Books

For more information you can view the Never Again website: https://www.narcissistic-abuse-recovery.com

ABOUT THE AUTHOR

Dr Sarah Davies is a Chartered Counselling Psychologist and Trauma Therapist with a private practice in Harley Street, London. In writing *Never Again* Dr. Sarah Davies draws from personal experience of Narcissistic Abuse and her own journey of recovery as well as from extensive clinical experience in the area of narcissistic abuse, codependency, echoism and related trauma.

www.drsarahdavies.com